KW-364-239

Charles Seale-Hayne Library
University of Plymouth
(01752) 588 588
LibraryandITenquiries@plymouth.ac.uk

WITHDRAWN
FROM
UNIVERSITY OF PLYMOUTH
LIBRARY SERVICES

EXETER COLLEGE OF ART LIBRARY

72 0007607 5
TELEPEN

Adolf Hitler's Third Reich was created to last for a thousand years, but it lasted in fact for twelve, from 1933 until the fall of Berlin in 1945. During its existence it plunged Europe into the useless slaughter of the Second World War, created an empire that covered most of the continent of Europe, and established a new and terrifying word—Nazism—with all its implications of totalitarianism, humiliation and inhumanity; and it created concentration camps and gas chambers, and in a few appalling years put to death more than six million innocent people.

This book traces the rise and fall of the Third Reich, and draws upon a wide range of contemporary evidence to build up an authentic picture of the Germany of the time. The author includes extracts from newspapers, diaries, novels and other sources to recreate the conditions of life for the middle classes, the rich and the poor, and the non-Aryan minorities. He deals, too, with topics such as the S.S., anti-Semitism and the Reich citizenship laws, the idea of *Lebensraum* and the impact of war on German society. The book closes with an account of the final reckoning for the leaders of the Third Reich at the Nuremberg war trials. An addition to the WAYLAND DOCUMENTARY HISTORY SERIES, this title is illustrated with more than fifty photographs, cartoons and other graphic material.

The Third Reich

Michael Berwick

WAYLAND PUBLISHERS LONDON

1490A

943.086

7607

0-85340-152-7

EXETER COLLEGE OF ART LIBRARY 4/72

THE WAYLAND DOCUMENTARY HISTORY SERIES

MEDIEVAL PILGRIMS *Alan Kendall*

THE REFORMATION OF THE SIXTEENTH CENTURY *L. W. Cowie*

WITCHCRAFT *Roger Hart*

PLAGUE AND FIRE *L. W. Cowie*

THE AGE OF DICKENS *Patrick Rooke*

GLADSTONE AND DISRAELI *Patrick Rooke*

ORIGINS OF WORLD WAR ONE *Roger Parkinson*

THE GREAT DEPRESSION *Marion Yass*

ORIGINS OF WORLD WAR TWO *Roger Parkinson*

THE PILGRIM FATHERS *L. W. Cowie*

THE HOME FRONT *Marion Yass*

Frontispiece A Jewish boy emerging from the Jewish ghetto in Warsaw, Poland after it was over-run by the Germans in 1943

SBN 85340 152 7
Copyright © 1971 by Wayland (Publishers) Ltd.
101 Grays Inn Road London WC1
Printed by The Garden City Press Limited,
Pixmore Avenue, Letchworth, Herts. SG6 1JS

Contents

The Illustrations

Introduction

MANY OF THE EVENTS described in this book are of an horrific nature. Some of them are records of oppression, violence, tyranny and murder calculated on a massive scale. Even to a generation raised on newsreel film of atrocities in Vietnam, Africa, and elsewhere, the political acts of Hitler's Third Reich (1933-45) hold a chilling sense of evil; here was a regime that legalized the destruction of an entire race of people, that created a vast machine for the purpose of human destruction, and that operated it with the cold logic of a railway timetable.

In many ways the history of the Third Reich is a history of frenzy and lunacy. Any regime that flaunts the concept of *Untermenschen*—subhuman species—and sets about, equipped with a perverse series of statutes and laws, to obliterate such a species, surely travels beyond the frontiers of sanity. Corruption, deceit, a basic disregard for human needs and feelings, the imposition of terror—these were the weapons of the German Reich that were used, with such repercussive effects, upon the enemies of Germany.

In some ways the history of the Third Reich reflects a general malaise of civilized society. There was a retreat to the barbarism of the Dark Ages, a breakdown in a sophisticated social system that permitted open violence and that led ultimately to the crematoria of Auschwitz and the so-called secret scientific experiments of the concentration camps—when human flesh was dried and bleached and turned into lampshades in the name of some perverted idea of progress.

That such things should happen in the middle of the twentieth century is almost beyond belief.

1 *Adolf Hitler and the Third Reich*

Nazi terror

THE THIRD REICH of Germany was designed to last for a thousand years. In the event Adolf Hitler's dictatorship lasted a little over twelve—from January, 1933, until April, 1945, when faced with the Russian assault upon Berlin the Führer (leader) killed himself in the cellar of the Berlin Chancellery. His mistress Eva Braun died with him.

Twelve short years—but they had seen the whole continent of Europe encompassed by flame and the destruction of war; they had witnessed German armies march across nations, flattening them into submission as if they had never existed; they had seen a whole new vocabulary of terror grow up—Nazism, concentration camps, the S.S. It was an apocalyptic time for Europe, an age from which it has hardly yet recovered.

The architect of the Third Reich, Adolf Hitler, was born in Braunau on the River Inn in Austria on 20th April, 1889. The future Führer's father was the illegitimate child of a man called Schickelgrüber, who was employed as a cook in a household in the town of Graz. Between the humble circumstances of his birth and the disintegrating grandeur of his death, Hitler achieved a very special place in history.

Hitler in Vienna

As a young man Hitler had pretensions towards becoming an artist. His talents did not seem to match his ambitions in this respect, and he was rejected by the Academy of Fine Arts in Vienna. He eked out a meagre living as a street artist and lived in a charity house. A description from this period exists of Hitler: "From under a greasy black derby hat, his hair hung long over his coat collar and a thick ruff of fluffy beard encircled his chin (1)."

The period of his life spent in Austria was one of bitterness and contempt. Later, when he looked back upon this time before the First World War he wrote: "Even today the mention of Vienna arouses only gloomy thoughts in my mind. Five years of poverty

Opposite top Adolf Hitler, the future leader of Germany, aged ten, and *bottom* the house in Braunau, Austria (cart outside) where he was born (1889)

in that town of Phaecians. Five years in which, first as a casual labourer, and then as a humble painter, I had to earn my daily bread. And a meagre morsel it was, not even enough to still my constant hunger (2)."

Hitler also encountered his first Jew in Vienna. This was an experience that was to stay with him and influence the later course of the Nazi genocide programme: "I suddenly encountered a phenomemon in a long caftan and wearing black sidelocks. My first thought was: is this a Jew? The longer I gazed at this strange countenance and examined it piece by piece, the more the question shaped itself in my brain: is this a German? . . . For the first time in my life I bought some anti-Semitic pamphlets for a few pence (3)."

Hitler's rabid anti-Semitism was toughened by his frustrating experiences in Vienna when he seemed to fail at everything he undertook. His views were expressed characteristically in his book *Mein Kampf (My Struggle):* "The Jews were responsible for bringing negroes into the Rhineland with the ultimate idea of bastardizing the white race which they hate and thus lowering its cultural and political level so that the Jew might dominate (4)." It was this garbled anti-Jewishness (see Chapter 4) which was to have such monstrous repercussions during the war years.

Corporal Hitler

In August, 1914, at the outbreak of the First World War, Hitler volunteered for a Bavarian regiment and was accepted. At last, he seemed to have found a niche for himself: "No words of mine can describe the satisfaction I felt: within a few days I was wearing that uniform I was not to put off again for nearly six years (5)."

Hitler's war service was restricted to the task of *Meldegänger* (messenger), carrying messages between Company and Regimental Headquarters. Undeniably brave, he was awarded the Iron Cross, Second Class. But wars have to end, and it was the end of the war that Hitler—then a corporal—most feared. What was he to do next?

Germany's surrender to the Allies in 1918 was a traumatic experience for him: "Everything went black before my eyes as I staggered back and buried my aching head between my blankets and pillow . . . The following days were terrible to bear and the nights still worse . . . (6)." What was he to do? Was he to remain

Facing page Kaiser William II of Germany (centre) and one of the German generals, Moltke (right), at the front, October 1914

"one of those everlasting barrack dwellers who don't know where else to go, a lance corporal with a lean, yellow, crabbed face, who wore the Iron Cross (7)?"

Political apprentice

He went to Munich, the city where he felt he most belonged. It was a Munich reeling under the shattering experience of defeat; the streets were filled with the grey masses of beaten German armies drifting home from the front. Hitler's introduction into politics came *via* the German Labour Party, founded by Anton Drexler and Karl Harrer. It soon came to Drexler's attention that Hitler "had the gift of the gab and could be used (8)."

Hitler attended meetings of the Party and made his first public

Political unrest was common in post-war Germany: this is a demonstration in Berlin

speech on 16th October, 1919, in the Hofbraukeller, a Munich beer hall: "I spoke for thirty minutes and what I had always felt deep down in my heart, without being able to test it, proved to be true. I could make a good speech (9)."

Following this, Hitler went from success to success as a public political speaker: "The lecturer gave a talk on Jewry. He showed that wherever one looked one saw Jews. The whole of Germany is governed by Jews. The Jew has money in his hands. He sits in the government and swindles and cheats ... Germans, be united against the Jews. The lecturer's last words: 'We shall carry on the struggle until the last Jew has been removed from Germany even

Members of the Socialist "Spartacist" Party, in Berlin, 1919, during the time of political unrest

if it comes to revolution.' The speaker received great applause (10)."

These were prophetic words. Sometimes, in reports, we can glimpse Hitler's demonstrative, riveting, volatile personality: "He got into such a rage that people at the back couldn't understand very much. During Herr Hitler's speech one man kept shouting 'Shame!' . . . and he was thrown out of the hall (11)."

Nazi Party

By 1920 the German Labour Party had changed its name to the National Socialist German Workers' Party, the "Nazis" for short;

Hitler held the reins very much in control. The Nazis' membership numbered 3,000. Soon Hitler was surrounded by a clique of undesirable people later to become notorious, or infamous, for their roles in the history of the Third Reich. Hermann Goering, later Reich Marshal; Rudolf Hess, the only one of the Nazi hierarchy imprisoned to this day in Spandau Jail in West Berlin; Max Amann, later to be the Nazi Party's publisher; and Alfred Rosenberg, one of the so-called creators of Nazi racial policy.

Hitler (left) and others enjoy comfortable conditions at Landsberg prison after Hitler's bid for power in Munich (1923)

The Munich Putsch

In 1923 came Hitler's ill-fated Munich *putsch*, or bid for power. At the head of a large crowd, Hitler tried to declare a seizure of power from the Bavarian Government. In the Odeonplatz the crowd was fired upon by a police cordon and sixteen people fell dead. (The nearby Feldherrnhalle later became a National Socialist shrine, permanently guarded by S.S. men.) Hitler was thrown into prison, and then put on trial. In his defence speech, he said he was prepared to be a martyr for the Germany that lost the war: "The court will judge us as Germans who only wanted the good of their own people and Fatherland, who wanted to fight and die. Pronounce us guilty a thousand times over: the goddess of the eternal court of history will smile and tear to pieces the State Prosecutor's submission and the court's verdict: for she acquits us (12)."

The trial was enough to spread Hitler's name, not only throughout the Weimar Republic of Germany, but across the pages of the world's newspapers. For those who wanted it, here at last was the Führer Germany had been waiting for, as religious fanatics will await a messiah. The racialist philosopher Houston Stewart Chamberlain, whose writings influenced much of Nazi thought, said: "The fact that at the hour of her deepest need Germany has given birth to a Hitler proves her vitality (13)."

Germany's messiah

Kurt Hesse had been dreaming of such a messiah in his book *Feldherr Psychologos*, in 1922: "Where he comes from, no one can say. From a prince's palace, perhaps, or a labourer's cottage. But everyone knows: He is the Führer. Everyone cheers him and he will one day announce himself, he for whom all of us are waiting, full of longing, who feel Germany's present distress deep in our hearts, so that thousands and hundreds of thousands of brains picture him, millions of voices call for him, one single German soul seeks him."

An almost religious fervour lay behind the plea. Hitler was the man the vanquished Germany had been waiting for. Behind the messianic impulse lay many causes. The defeat of the First World War had shocked the mighty German nation with its proud military past; the humiliation of the Treaty of Versailles had stripped Germany of what she felt to be many of her basic rights—such as having her own Air Force; a hugely inflated economy made the *Deutschmark* worthless paper; massive unemployment; bitterness and discontent on the part of the soldiers of the defeated German armies. The age was ripe for a Hitler. Leaders of the German Republic—men like Gustav Stresemann—seemed to have failed the nation.

In the twenties the German mark plummetted in value. Millions of pieces of worthless currency were printed and armfuls of notes were needed for even the smallest transaction

The year 1929 saw the great financial collapse on Wall Street in the United States; the waves of economic depression quickly spread to Europe. Between 1929 and 1932 unemployment in Germany rose from 1·3 millions to 5·1 millions; interest rates on loans had doubled from those of before the war; food prices were twice as high in Germany as elsewhere; savings were wiped out entirely by inflation. The result, by 1932, was a country brought to its knees and gasping for first aid. Struggling against the German Communists and other parties, the Nazis began to win great electoral victories.

By 1933, Hitler and his National Socialist Party were firmly in power. Not content with being Chancellor or President, Hitler had declared himself Führer or "leader." The German nation had been given a sense of purpose. It may have been a purpose that it disliked in many ways, but it made a strong appeal to patriotism and a new awakening: "the miracle of Germany's emergence as a nation (14)." Hitler could now be seen as the saviour, as a sorcerer

Poster for Reichstag election 1933, showing the "field-marshal" (Hindenberg) and the lance-corporal" (Hitler): "fight with us for peace and equality" says the caption

Dr. Josef Goebbels, who was in charge of Nazi propaganda

The Reichstag (German Parliament) building was sabotaged by the Nazis (1933), and blamed on the Communists in order to boost Hitler's power

or a magician, bolstered up by a growing propaganda machine masterminded by Josef Goebbels.

Nazi methods

Even so, none of the aura of hero-worship surrounding the Führer could disguise the fact that the Nazi regime was fundamentally totalitarian. Political opponents were rounded up and imprisoned. On the night of 27th February, 1933, the Reichstag (Parliament) in Berlin was set on fire, and the Nazis had a new excuse to retaliate against Communists and other left-wing activists.

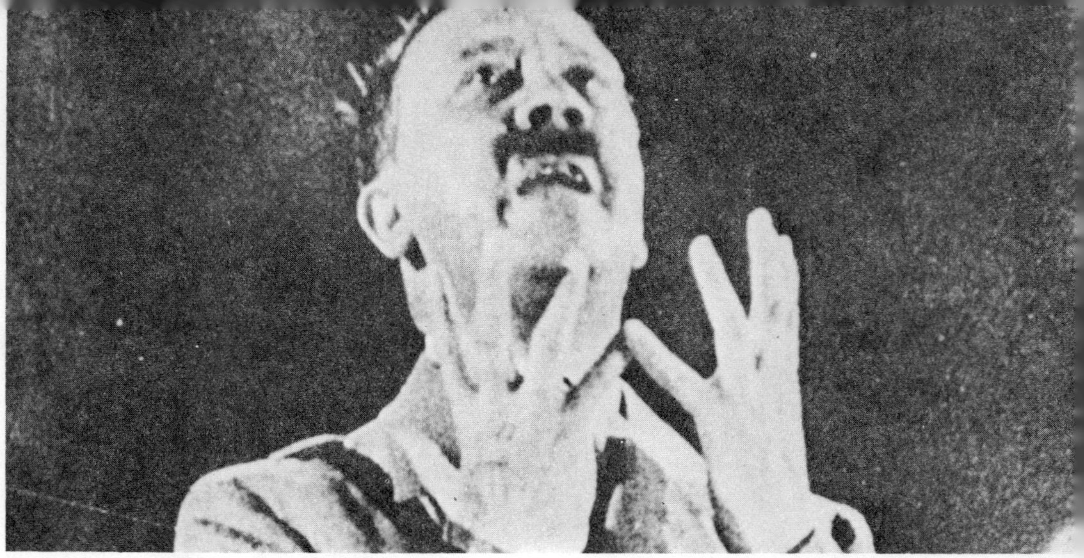

The next day, Hitler issued a decree, ostensibly a defensive measure against Communist acts of violence. In fact, it was a curtailment of individual liberty: "Restrictions on personal liberty, on the right of free expression of opinion, including freedom of the Press; on the rights of assembly and association; violations of the privacy of postal, telegraphic and telephonic communications; warrants for house searches; orders for confiscation as well as restrictions on property—are permissible beyond the legal limits otherwise prescribed (15)." In other words, Hitler was taking away several of the basic human rights that most civilized societies take for granted.

Worse still, Hermann Goering published an order which established a special auxiliary police force: 50,000 men were called up, 40,000 of them drawn from the ranks of the S.A. (Stormtroopers) and the S.S. (see Chapter 2). By simply putting a white arm-band over their brown or black shirts they became invested with police powers.

The Nazi regime established itself quickly and ominously, and yet for most ordinary Germans—whether voluntarily or under pressure—it seemed clear that these acts were only being done for the good of Germany. Because of the almost supernatural aspects of his power the Führer seemed infallible. Quite irrational beliefs surrounded this awestruck admiration of the Führer.

Hitler's personality

At the Nuremberg Olympic Games of 1936, for example, it was agreed that Hitler's appearance had been the omen for a German victory. A photograph showing Hitler bending over the hand of the acress Olga Tshechowa, brought her a flood of congratulatory letters: "It is good to know that you will marry Adolf Hitler," and "Make him happy—he deserves it (16)." His mystical *persona* penetrated almost every aspect of the Third Reich: "Hitler loves every member of the German nation and forgives each one of them everything that is humanly fallible. He loves you and me. He loves the whole German people and it is this love that forces them all towards him (17)." It might almost be a reference to an all-forgiving God!

Hitler's personal magnetism seems to have affected all classes of people: "Hitler entered the hall and was tempestuously hailed by his numerous followers among the students . . . His appearance

Opposite Three examples of Hitler's dramatic speaking style suprised me. On posters and in caricatures I had seen him in military tunic . . . but here he was wearing a well-fitted blue suit and looking remarkably respectable . . . As the ovation went on for minutes he tried, as if slightly pained, to check it . . . His initial silence soon disappeared; at times now his pitch rose. He spoke urgently and with hypnotic persuasiveness . . . I was carried on the wave of enthusiasm which, one could almost feel this physically, bore the speaker along from sentence to sentence . . . He seemed to feel that he was expressing what the audience, by now transformed into a single mass, expected of him . . . Afterward . . . I felt I had to straighten things out in my own mind, to master my confusion. Shaken, I drove off into the night (18)."

The Führer

For Rudolf Hess, Hitler was "the one man who remains beyond all criticism." Hess's devotion was complete: "Hitler is always right, and he will always be right. The National Socialism of all of us is anchored in uncritical loyalty, in the surrender to the Führer, in the silent execution of his orders. We believe that the Führer is obeying a higher call to shape German History. There can be no criticism of this belief (19)."

Even a leading churchman, Cardinal Faulhaber, wrote to the Vatican after a visit to Hitler: "He can be solemn and almost soft . . . The Chancellor, there is no doubt, lives in a state of belief in God (20)." Hitler's powers, his personal magnetism, were seemingly fathomless. How else could he have risen from the poverty and obscurity of Vienna to his position as divine ruler of the German nation?

Hitler's effect on ordinary people was considerable: "You kept seeing posters with the sun rising and there was a swastika in it. But a lot of people couldn't answer the question about where the sun rises, they didn't even know the right answer . . . My impression was that the people were simply dying for a change. The change was Hitler and the people liked him (21)."

The infallibility of the Führer was believed in by the lower classes as much as those of other classes who supported the Nazi regime: "In 1938 we had yet another proof of our Führer's infallible judgement, in his amazing knowledge of the feeling and tempers of those outside as well as inside Germany. When our Army marched into Austria, there was little to indicate how it would be received. One could not help wondering if there would be bloodshed, but the Führer knew. Our troops were received with open arms, they were pelted with flowers (22)."

Amongst young people Hitler had a special effect: "Gradually one after the other the old schoolmasters were weeded out. The new masters who replaced them were young men loyal to the Führer. The new spirit had come to stay. We obeyed orders, and we acknowledged the leadership principle because we wanted to and because we liked it . . . In the spring of 1939 I met Adolf Hitler personally—face to face. It was a lucky accident—perhaps more than that. I think it must have been my destiny once in my life to see my Führer and speak to him (23)."

Hitler instilled Nazism as early as possible in a child's life

Hitler with early members of the Nazi party; Goering, later head of the German air force, on his right

Hitler and the Army

By 1934 Hitler was not only Chancellor (equivalent to Prime Minister) but also Head of State on the death of the old President Hindenburg; he also appointed himself Commander-in-Chief of the Armed Forces. He had assumed absolute power and the Nazi Party could now penetrate the high ranks of the *Wehrmacht* (Army). In January, 1936, General Dollmann, Commander of *Wehrkreis* IX, issued the following directive: it shows the *official* attitude of the *Wehrmacht* to the Führer and the Party: "The officer corps must have confidence in the representatives of the party. Party opinions should not be examined or rejected . . . Decisions from high Party Headquarters are *official* and therefore *binding* for us. In order to show outwardly a positive attitude towards the Party, I want attention paid to the following points (24):

(a) in every officers' mess worthy pictures of the Führer and Supreme Commander are to be displayed in a prominent place.
(b) No functions are to be held in officers' messes by groups which are disapproved of by the Party.
(c) Talks may be given only by people without political bias, and who will speak in a National Socialist sense.
(d) It is desired that the wives of officers take an active part in the National Socialist League of Women. In conversations off-duty, officers must always show a positive attitude towards National Socialism."

Opposite The military precision and gigantic scale of a Nazi rally. Hitler on the dais

Hitler Youth, the youth group of the Nazi party, in camp

Lebensraum

As Commander-in-Chief the Führer now had the military controls of Germany firmly at his fingertips. Besides, power over the Army suited his future plans. Later he was to talk about *Lebensraum* (living space) and the idea of German expansion into other parts of Europe: "The history of all ages had proved that expansion could only be carried out by breaking down resistance and taking risks; setbacks were inevitable. There had never been spaces without a master, and there were none today. The attacker always comes up against a possessor. The question for Germany ran: where could she achieve the greatest gain at the lowest cost (25)." This argument of *Lebensraum* was to support his later moves against Austria and Czechoslovakia (see Chapter 3).

Life in the Reich

Life in the Third Reich was now life under a restrictive dictatorship. Democratic elections had ceased to exist, and a Secret Police organization (see Chapter 2) had access to the private lives and activities of individuals. Fear prevented possible opponents from speaking out too loudly against the regime. What then was the

Hitler Youth trumpeters at a meeting

texture of life like? How did people live?

If you were an opponent of the regime, you could express your feelings and discover your friends only in the most secret of ways: "I find that it does not take long to spot people who think as one does oneself. They do not talk about the 'Führer' but about 'Hitler', they despise the 'House of German Art' and the art displayed there. They read Jakob Burckhardt and Spengler, English novels and French lyric poetry . . . they prefer chamber music to Wagner's operas and steer clear of Party meetings and parades. They switch off the radio when Hitler's speeches are broadcast, listen to British stations and speak of rationing and petrol shortage in a peculiarly pessimistic manner. I dare say that *agents provocateurs* do the same thing but they are usually more clumsy about it (26)."

Denunciations

To oppose the Nazi government brought the risk of denunciation. No-one was to be trusted, from a next-door neighbour to a young member of the Hitler Youth. Instances of sons denouncing fathers were not unknown, nor of uncles denouncing nephews. The

Gestapo (see Chapter 2), that all-hearing ear and all-seeing eye of the Nazi party, had an alarming ubiquitous quality. A leading Viennese dancer received a prison sentence for listening to foreign radio broadcasts—denounced by his own daughter. In Berlin in 1934 a schoolboy caused his own father to be imprisoned by interrupting the anti-Jewish tirade of his schoolteacher with the words, "My Daddy says Jews are not damnably vile (27)."

Abuse of power

Most Germans supported the regime and obeyed orders, in accordance with Foreign Minister von Ribbentrop: "We Germans are a peculiar people; we are so loyal (28)." For them, life in the Third Reich entailed acceptance of acts of terror, deportations, loss of liberty, and other gross abuses of power. At another level it meant accepting Nazi censorship of the kind of plays you saw, the films you saw, the books you read, the music you listened to, the newspapers you took. Failure to comply with Nazi instructions brought dark threats. A circular was sent out with the newspaper the *Fränkische Tageszeitung*, which illustrates this point exactly: "Our paper certainly deserves the support of every German. We shall continue to forward copies of it to you and hope that you will not want to expose yourself to unfortunate consequences in the case of cancellation (29)."

Women's rights

In every sense, then, the Third Reich meant a life of restricted freedom. It entailed compulsory adulation of Adolf Hitler and acceptance of Nazi doctrine, and created inroads into ordinary human liberty. This is especially true in connection with the status of women in Hitler's Germany. Women were excluded from all leading positions in the Party hierarchy. After 1933, married women doctors and civil servants were dismissed from their posts, and the numbers of women high-school teachers declined drastically. From 1936, women could no longer act as judges or public prosecutors and were ineligible for jury service.

According to Goebbels, "Woman has the task of being beautiful and bringing children into the world (30)," and Hitler put it that, "Woman has her battlefield too, with each child she brings for the nation, she is fighting her fight on behalf of the nation (31)." Hitler even wanted to stake a personal claim in each child: "Children belong to their mothers as at the same moment they belong to me (32)." So women were relegated to the kitchen and to pains of childbirth.

Ernst Kaltenbrunner of the S.S. proclaimed: "All single and married women up to the age of thirty-five who do not already have four children should be obliged to produce four children by racially pure, unexceptionable German men. Whether these men are married is without significance. Every family that already has four children must set the husband free for this action (33)." Precisely how women were to bring up fatherless children is not explained.

By 1939, when many of Germany's young men were at war, S.S. Reichsführer Heinrich Himmler had conceived the idea of setting up the *Lebensborn*. This was a place where young women of Aryan stock could meet young men of similar descent for the purpose of procreating children. Without such offspring "we shall not be able to maintain the Great Germanic Empire that is in the process of coming into existence (34)." In an odd sense, women had been demoted to a status that resembled that of the Jews within the Third Reich (see Chapter 4).

A state of fear

In less than twelve years, Hitler had managed to create within Germany itself a repressive totalitarian state in which only those of pure Aryan descent could be first-class citizens, and only then if they were of the male sex. He had deprived a civilization of its basic liberties, and had put in their place a society based upon fear, control and violence. If he had also given the German nation a new sense of patriotism, and had restored vitality to the people, then these are surely outweighed by the great costs that were to come later.

Perhaps Hitler himself is the best spokesman for what the Third Reich meant: "The selection of the new Führer class is what my struggle for power means. Whoever proclaims his allegiance to me is, by this very proclamation . . . one of the chosen. This is the great significance of our long, dogged struggle for power, that in it will be born a new master class, chosen to guide the fortunes not only of the German people but of the world (35)."

The contrasting uniforms of the S.A. (left) and S.S. (right)

2 The S.S.

THE ABBREVIATION S.S. comes from the word *Schutzstaffel,* which literally means "bodyguard." The S.S. was formed in 1925 for the prime purpose of protecting Adolf Hitler. In 1929, Heinrich Himmler took charge of its organization, and under his control it grew during the 1930s until it had permeated every aspect of German life—police, security, the army, the concentration camps. It became, quite literally, a state within a state. *Schutzstaffel*

From the very outset it was obvious that the S.S. was to be a mythic part of German life, and Himmler—selecting his members chiefly from those of Aryan descent—incorporated quasi-legendary qualities into the concept of the S.S. The uniform was black, the jackboots were of black leather, and the caps were decorated with the skull, the death's head symbol. And bound up with the idea was something of the elements of the legendary Teutonic Knights. Even the oath of honour, sworn by each S.S. cadet, had a religious, mystical ring to it (36):

I swear to thee Adolf Hitler
As Führer and Chancellor of the German Reich
Loyalty and Bravery.
I vow to thee and to the superiors of your choosing
Obedience unto death
So help me God.

Contained in the oath are ideas that were to be an inherent part of S.S. discipline—loyalty, bravery, and obedience. Without these a man could not possibly hope to become a member of the S.S. Another idea often referred to in the picture of the "ideal" S.S. man is that of hardness. For example, the statement of Odilo Globocnik, chief of the S.S. in German occupied Poland: "If a generation should ever follow us that is so spineless and weak-kneed as not to *S.S. hardness*

understand our great task, then National Socialism shall indeed have been in vain. On the contrary, I am of the opinion that bronze tablets should be laid recording that we had the courage to carry out this great and so necessary work (37)."

"The great and necessary work" referred to here was a description of the concentration camps (see Chapter 5). Heinrich Himmler himself spoke of hardness in a very similar context: "Most of you will know what it means when a hundred corpses are lying side by side, when five hundred are lying there or when a thousand are lying there. To have stuck this out and at the same time—apart from exceptions due to human weaknesses—to have remained decent, that is what has made us hard (38)." The use of the word "decent" in this context is impossible to understand. But the need for hardness was a definite prerequisite of any self-respecting S.S. member, the more so when his work entailed mass extermination.

S.S. training

The rank-and-file S.S. member had toughness drilled into him: "There was a special method of humiliating a man. If anyone, while filling cartridges into a charger, let a cartridge fall to the ground, he had to pick it up with his teeth. I made up my mind that I would not do that. They can do what they like with me, I said, but I will not pick up a cartridge with my teeth: I shall use my hand . . . One day of course it happened. I bent down and picked the cartridge up with my hand. The N.C.O. rushed at me like a wild animal. 'Chuck that cartridge away,' was his first order. I threw the cartridge away. It fell some six feet away from me. I was almost at the stage of picking it up with my teeth. But then—I don't know why—I picked it up with my hand.

"That really did it! He went scarlet . . . [He ordered me] to do fifty knees-bend with rifle held out at arm's length. I had to count out loud . . . After twenty knees-bend I stopped counting. I just couldn't go on. I lowered my rifle and I stood up. I felt I had to weep . . . When he saw this he bellowed: 'Mollycoddle! Mother's little darling! Crybaby! Who ever heard of an S.S. man blubbering!' . . . He ordered me to clean out all the first floor latrines for a week. [The next time] he ordered me to throw a cartridge away I did so and then without even waiting I picked it up with my teeth . . . (39)."

Humiliation was one way of hardening an S.S. man. Yet given the sorts of disgusting jobs that the S.S. were expected to carry out,

Opposite Tough training instilled the required hardness in S.S. soldiers hardness was clearly a protective shell. The following is a good example, written by an S.S. man in occupied Poland: "Our commander (sometimes) took ten or twenty men from the unsuspecting population and had them hanged. Every time he ordered me 'Get a gallows ready'—you can imagine how shattered I was when I heard this order for the first time. I said to him, 'Sturmbannführer, I ask you to release me from this order.' He merely said: 'Milksop! And you want to be an S.S. man!' I had to carry out the order (40)."

Waffen-S.S.

Of course, not all branches of the S.S. were involved in the Polish extermination camps. This was a task reserved for the so-called *Totenkopfverbände,* or Death's Head units. The S.S., like some monstrous black river, had many tributaries. There was for example the *Waffen-S.S.,* the fighting arm of the organization, which grew in size from 100,000 men in 1940 to 900,000 by 1944. The same hard pride seemed to exist throughout the S.S. regardless of the branch.

Members of the *Waffen-S.S.* did, however, disregard any connection with the Death's Head units: "It was hard for the Americans to realize that there was a difference between S.S. and *Waffen-S.S.* They put us all in the same boat. They got the *Waffen-S.S.* mixed up with the Death's Head units and the concentration camp guards. But we had nothing to do with those guys (41)."

These are the words of a former *Waffen-S.S.* man, wrongly arrested by the Americans after Germany's defeat in 1945. It is interesting to note, in the same context, that although *Waffen-S.S.* reunions are held regularly in Germany today, and although there exists a Mutual Aid Organization called *Hilfsorganisation auf Gegenseitigkeit* (H.I.A.G.) for former *Waffen-S.S.* men, the same man could say: "We don't accept anybody in the H.I.A.G. who was a concentration camp guard. We don't take anybody from the Death's Head units. We don't want anything to do with those guys . . . (42)."

S.S. power

Looking back it is clear that great distinctions existed within the S.S. It will be useful to mention just how far, at the peak of its power, the S.S. had broken into different segments of German life and how far it managed to permeate them.

Amongst S.S. responsibilities were the following: marriage authorizations, certificates of birth and ancestry, a supreme police court, fire brigades, colonial police, and establishments for political education. This is to say nothing of the concentration camps and the notorious Gestapo—the *Geheime Staatspolizei* or Secret State Police. Of all S.S. activity it was that of the Gestapo which produced most dread in the German population at large.

The Gestapo

Situated at Number 8, Prinz-Albrecht-Strasse in Berlin—an address that was horribly meaningful to every German—the Gestapo was set up in April, 1933, to deal with "political police tasks." By 1936 the Prussian Gestapo was authorized "to investigate and suppress all anti-State tendencies throughout Prussia, to assemble and evaluate the results of any unrest." This authority placed in Gestapo hands an inordinate amount of power.

Ursula von Kardorff, a journalist in wartime Berlin, typified the general dread of the Gestapo that existed at the time: "At 6 p.m. I had a telephone call at the office. 'This is the S.S. Head Office. Please be here at ten o'clock tomorrow morning and report to Superintendent Opitz. We should like you to give us certain information.' So it's the Prinz-Albrecht-Strasse for me, the most sinister address in Berlin (43)."

And later: "Home again. I still cannot quite realize it! I was questioned for seven hours on end! And in the Prinz-Albrecht-Strasse, the Gestapo Headquarters. And yet I am free! I simply cannot grasp it (44)."

The force of Ursula's relief shows the sombre yet awful finality which people had come to associate with a visit to Gestapo Headquarters in Berlin. So many entered to face torture and death. It also indicates on the part of the average person in Germany an acceptance of the fact that the Gestapo, and the S.S. in general, was an intrinsic part of the fabric of German life.

The "blond god"

At least in its earliest years the S.S. was held to be the living symbol of Aryan manhood. Its members were carefully selected as good specimens of pure German blood. No one could have been more typical than Heinrich Himmler's second-in-command, Reinhardt Heydrich, known as the "blond God." Heydrich's career in many ways typifies the S.S. ideal. In 1931 he held the rank of *Untersturmführer* (lieutenant) but by 1934 he was chief of the Gestapo. By 1940 he had become President of the International Criminal Police Commission. He was later assassinated in Prague,

Reinhardt Heydrich, deputy to Himmler head of the S.S.

but even in death he projected the image to the extreme: "There can be no better proof of the iron discipline to which he subjected both himself and his body than the moments immediately after he had been attacked when, mortally wounded and in agonizing pain, he still mustered the strength to reach for his holster, open it, and send five shots after his attackers (45)."

Heydrich and Himmler

Heydrich's role in the S.S. hierarchy was almost mystical. Nicknamed not only "blond God" but "Mr. Suspicion," his motivation was a seemingly constant search for total power. It was a search that led him to a bitter—if disguised—contempt of Reichsführer Himmler. Their meetings often broke down with Himmler, having lost an argument to Heydrich, crying in despair: "You and your logic! We never hear about anything but your logic. Everything I propose you batter down with your logic. I'm fed up with you and your cold, rational cynicism (46)."

This regard for logic and rational argument, combined with his Aryan appearance and "sinister wolf's eyes (47)," is a fair case, at least superficially, for the argument that Heydrich was the very epitome of the S.S. man—in his detachment, his lack of passion, and even in his appearance. Even so, he could frequently be servile in his relationships with Himmler, although the servility has a clear sarcasm about it. Frequently he would address the Reichsführer thus: "Certainly, Herr Reichsführer, if that is the Herr Reichs-

A forbidding group of S.S. motor cyclists

führer's wish, I will have the necessary arrangements made at once and report back to the Herr Reichsführer (48)."

But this servility was simply part of Heydrich's ruthless ambition. He drove himself relentlessly to new and challenging heights of power. It was Heydrich who created the secret police agency known as the S.D. *(Sicherheitsdienst)* whose task it was to track down rebels or traitors within the National Socialist Party. In his Headquarters at Number 4, Zuccalistrasse in Munich, every report, every tiny detail was noted on an elaborate card-index system. Heydrich himself was once described as being "a living card-index, a brain which held all the threads and wove them together (49)." It was Heydrich who turned the S.D. into an exhaustive, cynical, and painstaking secret police.

The Röhm Putsch

If Heydrich's ruthlessness is in many ways typical of the S.S. ideal, what of the ruthlessness within the S.S. itself that was to earn a reputation for barbarism unsurpassed in the twentieth century? It is possible to isolate a turning point in the history of the S.S. when it not only established its own supremacy, but perpetrated a gross act of authorized and brutal assassination. The Röhm *Putsch*, or "the night of the long knives" as the killing is sometimes called, took place in June, 1934. It was a blood-bath that seemed to mark the decline of the S.S. into the acts of supreme terror it was later to commit.

Hitler with S.A. officers; Rohm, their leader, is immediately behind him

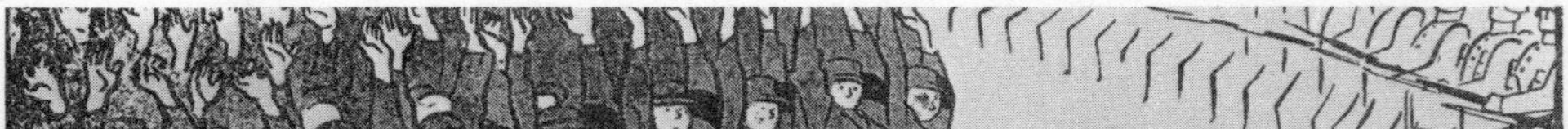

Cartoonist David Low's comment on "the night of the long knives", when many S.A. men, on the instructions of Himmler (head of the S.S.), were massacred

Rudolf Hess, Hitler's deputy (centre)

The "night of the long knives" was the final confrontation between the S.S.—represented by Heydrich and Himmler—and the S.A. (*Sturmabteilung*—stormtroopers, or Brown Shirts), who were the original bodyguards of the Nazi Party in 1921. For some time emnity had been growing between these rival organizations. The breaking-point was bound to be reached sooner or later. The leader of the S.A. was Ernst Röhm, a sexual pervert, who had frequently tiraded against Hitler himself: "Hitler is a traitor and at the very least must go on leave . . . If we can't get there with him, we'll get there without him (50)."

"Night of the long knives"

The scene of the final confrontation was Bad Wiessee, Röhm's holiday resort. During that fateful summer evening of 1934, Röhm was welcoming old friends to the local Hanselbauer Hotel. Savage murders were taking place elsewhere throughout Germany. While an S.S. detachment moved in towards Bad Wiessee to arrest Röhm, incidents of violence were already rolling on inexorably towards a bloody climax. S.S. assassins, authorized to settle old scores, killed their S.A. victims without mercy.

Even the fate of Ernst Röhm was the subject of some jealous haggling. Rudolf Hess and Max Amann, the Nazi Party publisher, both wanted the job. "My Führer, the duty to shoot Röhm is mine (51)," Hess is reported to have said. Six S.A. leaders were cold-bloodedly shot on Hitler's orders in Stadelheim Jail. Dr. Wilhelm Schmid was taken by the S.S. and a coffin sent to his family some time later from Dachau concentration camp with the order that it was to remain closed. The savaged body of Ritter von Kahr was found on open country near Dachau, mutilated by a pick-axe. General von Schleicher was gunned down at his office desk, and so was his wife. Röhm himself was shot three times in his cell and killed. Father Bernhard Stempfle, who helped to edit Hitler's *Mein Kampf*, was found in Harlaching forest, his neck broken, three shots in the heart.

Hitler unrepentant

The total number of murders will probably never be known. Estimates vary from as low as seventy-seven to as high as a thousand, although *The White Book of the Purge*, published in Paris, states that 401 had been assassinated. It was the first act of wanton barbarism of the Third Reich. It underlined the bloody character of Hitler's dictatorship, since now he could dispense with legality. In a speech in the Reichstag on 13th July, 1934, he said: "If anyone reproaches me and asks why I did not resort to the regular courts of justice then all I can say is this: In this hour I was responsible for the fate of the German people and thereby I became the supreme judge of the German people (52)."

From the viewpoint of the S.S., "the night of the long knives" established the organization firmly and finally in the German totalitarian hierarchy. More important still, it was awarded a strange and perverse form of promotion by the Führer: "In view of the great services rendered by the S.S., particularly in connection with the events of 30th June, 1934, I hereby promote the S.S. to the status of independent organization within the framework of the National Socialist Party (53)." So terror and murder were given the gloss of an official decree from Hitler himself. The violence of the Röhm Putsch was only a taste of what was yet to come.

The "storm columns"

It is difficult now to quite grasp the intricacies of the influence held by the S.S. at the peak of its power. It operated within every sphere of life in the Reich and at the same time it terrorized the whole German nation. It considered itself, according to Hauptsturmführer Wisliceny, "a new form of religious sect with its own rites and customs." For Heydrich it was "enveloped in the mysterious aura of the political detective story (54)." And S.S.—Reichsführer Himmler himself said, "I know that there are many in Germany who feel uncomfortable when they see this black tunic: we understand this and do not expect to be beloved (55)."

Even the sound of the words in an S.S. marching song manage to convey something of the chilling image (56):

Clear the streets, the S.S. marches
The storm-columns stand at the ready.
They will take the road
From tyranny to freedom.
So we are ready to give our all
As did our fathers before us.
Let death be our battle companion.
We are the Black Band.

At the end of the war the charges laid against the "Black Band" were almost impossible to imagine: the murder of six million Jews, two million Poles, half a million gipsies, half a million Russian prisoners of war. Never in this, or any other century, can an organization have dealt out such incredible horrors and stood so indicted.

"The S.S. was used for purposes which were criminal, brutalities and killings in concentration camps, the administration of the slave labour programme and the maltreatment and murder of prisoners of war (57)." That was the summary of the Allied judges at the Nuremberg War Crimes trial.

It is hard today for us to imagine the place that the S.S. held in the Germany of the Third Reich; or even to imagine the terror—the knock on the door in the dead of night, the people who vanished without trace, the horrible extermination camps at Chelmno, Auschwitz and Treblinka. What is certain is that the Third Reich could never have existed without the S.S.—and the converse is probably true as well.

To be an S.S. man in the Third Reich was to be above and beyond the ordinary laws of civilization and society. It was to belong to what Himmler himself called an "Order of Germanic clans."

3 War and Defeat

Anschluss

ON 13TH MARCH, 1938, the German army marched into neighbouring Austria, an event that has subsequently been called the *Anschluss* or "annexation" of Austria. It was an active demonstration of Hitler's policy of *Lebensraum*—living space for Germany. In Vienna cheering crowds lined the streets: many Austrians were themselves Nazi supporters.

In 1935 Hitler had declared to the Reichstag that "Germany neither intends nor wishes to interfere in the internal affairs of Austria, to annex Austria, or to conclude an *Anschluss* (58)." But a treaty was drawn up between the two countries in 1936 under which Schuschnigg, the Austrian Chancellor, made significant concessions to the Nazis; these included the release of more than 15,000 Nazi political prisoners in Austria. By 1938, Hitler's designs of the Rhineland area and its strategic value had gone beyond the stage of empty platitudes.

By 10th March, 1938, he had made his intentions clear: "If other measures prove unsuccessful, I intend to invade Austria with armed forces in order to establish constitutional conditions and to prevent further outrages against the pro-German population. The forces detailed must be ready on 12th March at the latest from midday. I reserve the right to decide the actual moment for invasion (59)."

The pretext for the invasion, if one was needed, was to aid brother Germans living in distress in Austria. On 12th March Hitler crossed the Austro-German border and delivered a speech in the town of Linz: "If Providence once called me forth from this town to be the leader of the Reich, it must have charged me with a mission, and that mission could only be to restore my beloved homeland to the German Reich (60)."

So it was that Austria became the first country to be brought under Nazi control, the first nation in the future German Empire.

Opposite German soldiers decorated with the Iron Cross for gallantry at the Western Front (1940)

In 1938 German soldiers marched into Austria

There can be no doubt of Austrian solidarity for Hitler: in the Austrian elections that took place in April following the *Anschluss* 99·75 per cent of the vote was behind Hitler. The annexation of Austria was the first action on the road to the Second World War (1939-45).

Austrian Nazis

The Austrian Nazis, licensed at long last by the Führer's possession of their homeland, committed terrible acts of brutality against the Jewish community: "There was an orgy of sadism. Day after day large numbers of Jewish men and women could be seen scrubbing Schuschnigg signs off the sidewalk . . . while they were working on their hands and knees with jeering storm troopers standing over them, crowds gathered to taunt them (61)."

In fact, thousands of Austrian Jews were jailed; their possessions were confiscated and many of them emigrated. While the railway stations of Vienna were packed with Jewish people trying to escape, thousands of others in sheer desperation and despair committed

Many Austrians supported Hitler; here people of Innsbruck salute German troops

suicide. The Austrian leader Kurt von Schuschnigg was imprisoned and only released from the notorious Dachau camp in 1945.

Czechoslovakia

If Austria toppled without resistance, how did Hitler's next conquest react? Czechoslovakia, which also shared a border with Germany, was the obvious target for his next move. Hitler felt he could invade her with impunity—since world reaction to the *Anschluss* had been barely raised above a simper of protest. If Austria began the road to war, Czechoslovakia led Europe up to the very frontiers of calamity.

Czechoslovakia was a different proposition from the Nazi-orientated Austria. It had an army and strong defences. It would certainly offer military resistance. But what was going to be the Führer's pretext this time?

The question was that of the Sudeten Germans, a Czech minority of more than three million people who wanted closer ties with the Fatherland and less interference from the Czech capital, Prague.

The issue of Home Rule for the Sudeten Germans dominated Czech-German relations before the Munich crisis.

Keitel's plan

By May, 1938, General Keitel (see Chapter 6) had issued the following military directive on Hitler's instructions: "It is not my intention to smash Czechoslovakia by military action in the immediate future . . . unless unavoidable developments within that country force the issue or political events in Europe create a favourable opportunity which may possibly never recur.

"Operations will be launched either: (a) after a period of increasing diplomatic controversies and tension which will be exploited so as to shift the war guilt on to the enemy; (b) by lightning action as the result of a serious incident which will subject Germany to unbearable provocation and which, in the eyes of at least a part of world opinion, affords a moral justification for military measure. Case (b) is more favourable both from a military and political point of view (62)."

The "moral justification" General Keitel speaks of sounds odd in this kind of directive. On 20th May an alarmed Czech Government, upset by growing discontent amongst the Sudeten Germans and reports of German troop concentrations near the border, ordered a partial mobilization of its forces. Yet on 23rd May the Czech Ambassador in Berlin was reassured that Germany had no military intentions toward his country; Konrad Henlein, the Sudeten German leader, resumed talks with Prague. Intense diplomatic negotiations took place in European capitals as Germany was urged to desist from any aggressive intent towards the Czechs—ultimately, of course, to no avail.

On 18th June the Führer issued a new directive. He would act against Czechoslovakia only if he were certain that France and England would not intervene. Unlike events in Austria, the Czech situation was arousing international concern.

On 12th September, 1938, Hitler spoke at the annual Nazi Party rally in Nuremberg in terms that were far from ambivalent: "A Great Power cannot suffer an encroachment upon its rights . . . The Germans in Czechoslovakia are neither defenceless nor are they deserted. And people should take notice of that fact (63)."

Chamberlain's message

The evening of the next day brought an urgent message from Neville Chamberlain, the British Prime Minister: "In view of the

Neville Chamberlain, the British Prime Minister who tried to prevent a war with Hitler

increasingly critical situation I propose to come over at once to see you with a view to finding a peaceful solution. I propose to come across by air and am ready to start tomorrow. Please indicate the earliest time at which you can see me and suggest place of meeting. I should be grateful for a very early reply (64)."

The conversation between the Führer and Neville Chamberlain took place on 15th September at Berchtesgaden, Hitler's country home. It was largely incommunicative. Chamberlain did however agree in principle to a secession of the Sudeten region of Czechoslovakia. In the meantime, Hitler had promised to take no military action. It is one of history's ironies that Chamberlain could report: "In spite of the hardness and ruthlessness I thought I saw in Hitler's face, I got the impression that here was a man who could be relied upon when he had given his word (65)." But Hitler broke his promise and forged ahead with the invasion plans.

Godesberg talks

By 22nd September Chamberlain again left for Germany. His conversation with Hitler at Godesberg was a slap in the face for the British Prime Minister. Chamberlain agreed that British, French and Czech governments would accept the transfer of the Sudetenland from Czechoslovakia to Germany, but was staggered to discover that Hitler found this idea unacceptable. The following day the Führer demanded evacuation of the ceded territory by the morning of 28th September. Later, however, Hitler offered a concession by putting the date back to 1st October. Chamberlain, feeling that this was at least a step in the right direction, returned home to London.

On 26th September, however, the Führer made a vitriolic speech in the Berlin Sportpalast: "Now two men stand arrayed against each other: there is Herr Benes [President of Czechoslovakia] and there is myself . . . In the great struggle of the peoples, while Herr Benes was sneaking through the world, I as a decent German soldier did my duty . . . With regard to the problem of Sudeten Germans my patience is now at an end . . . The decision now lies in Herr Benes' hands: Peace or War. He will either accept my offer and give the [Sudeten] Germans their freedom, or we will go and fetch this freedom for ourselves . . . I have never been a coward. Now I go before my people as its first soldier . . . We are determined! (66)."

In his *Berlin Diary,* William Shirer observed of his speech: "For the first time in all the years I've observed him, he seemed tonight to have completely lost control of himself . . . . He slumped into his chair exhausted (67)."

Munich crisis

On 29th September, 1938, while Europe hovered on the brink of war, Chamberlain returned to Germany yet again, this time to the ill-fated Munich conference. When it was over Chamberlain returned to London, in an all too brief triumph, brandishing his infamous piece of paper, a text signed both by Hitler and himself: "We, the German Führer and the British Prime Minister, have had a further meeting today and are agreed in recognizing that the question of Anglo-German relations is of the first importance for the two countries and for Europe. We regard the agreement signed last night and the Anglo-German Naval Agreement as symbolic of the desire of our two peoples never to go to war with one another again . . . (68)."

Less than six months later—on 15th March, 1939—German troops had invaded Czechoslovakia. The Czech nation ceased to exist. By 1st September, 1939, the Germans had invaded Poland. England issued an ultimatum. The Second World War had begun.

Barely a country in the world did not in some way suffer from

Above In despair a Czech woman is forced to give a Nazi salute its effects. It could surely never have been predicted that such widespread conflicts would follow the German armies' invasion of Poland.

Germans in Poland

Nor was Germany's conquest of Poland achieved within the limits of the conventions of war. That unfortunate country was subjected to barbarism on a hitherto unknown scale: ruthless Nazi police methods were put into effect and public executions were a common sight in Warsaw and other cities.

It took one week from the entry into Poland for the Polish army

German soldier and gun symbolize occupied Poland

to be smashed by the overwhelming strength of the Germans. The Polish Army lost 200,000 men in the course of the fighting (69) while their leaders fled from the country to continue the resistance from afar. Worse was to follow for the Polish nation. It was not enough that they had been invaded by the German armies in the West; on 17th September Russian forces—allied to Germany in the so-called Pact of Steel—crossed the Polish frontiers to the East. Poland was then torn apart with comparatively few casualties for the German forces.

Here is an account of a man who took part in the entry into Poland: "We loaded our tanks and trucks on to the train and travelled for three days to Paprad in Slovakia, where we waited about ten miles from the Polish border . . . At dawn we crossed into Poland. There was virtually no resistance . . . We passed hundreds of Polish troops walking dejectedly towards Slovakia. The Poles seemed to be completely apathetic and there were so many prisoners that nobody bothered to guard them or even tell them where to go (70)."

Phoney war

But if Poland had fallen, what was happening in the West? What were the French going to do, faced with a darkening threat of military Germany to the East? After the fall of Poland, in fact, there began the period known as the "phoney war" when very little of military consequence took place: the Germans called it the *Sitzkrieg*—the "sitting-down war." In fact, the Allies were ill-prepared for military action of the kind needed to halt any further German attacks. The British had sent troops to France in case of a German invasion there, but their number was derisory: 158,000 men.

Would the war have turned out differently if the Allies had been able to attack Germany's exposed Western flank while the Polish campaign was being waged? The answer might well be yes: "The success against Poland was possible only by baring our Western border. If the French had seen the logic of the situation and had used the engagement of German forces in Poland, they would have been able to cross the Rhine . . . (71)."

According to General Keitel: "We had always expected an attack by the French during the Polish campaign and were very surprised that nothing happened (72)."

By 10th October Hitler was pushing his war aims a little further. After a largely rhetorical plea for peace in Europe, he issued his Top Secret Directive No. 6—preparations for an attack on Luxembourg, Holland and Belgium were to be undertaken without delay. Northern France was another military target, one which would afford great strategic value against England.

Weser Exercize

But Hitler's attentions were turned also to the occupation of Norway and Denmark. In January, 1940, preparations were made for this "Weser Exercize" as it was called. By March a directive was issued and the stage was set for Germany's occupation of Scandinavia. Here is a part of the Führer's directive: "The development of the situation in Scandinavia requires preparations to be made for the occupation of Denmark and Norway. This operation should prevent British encroachment on Scandinavia and the Baltic . . . In view of our military and political power in comparison with that of the Scandinavian countries, the force to be employed in the 'Weser Exercize' will be kept as small as possible . . . It is most important that the Scandinavian states should be taken by surprise (73)."

By early April the first ships of the occupation had set sail for Scandinavia—disguised! Secret commands laid down this order of subterfuge: "All ships must be darkened . . . The disguise as British craft must be kept as long as possible (74)."

Simultaneously, German troops marched into the two countries and an ultimatum was handed to the governments of Norway and Denmark: "German troops do not set foot on Norwegian soil as enemies . . . On the contrary, German military operations aim exclusively at protecting the north against the proposed occupation

A German Heinkel plane patrols a Norwegian fiord; Norway fell to Germany in 1940

of Norwegian bases by Anglo-French forces. The Reich government therefore expects that the Norwegian government and the people will offer no resistance. Resistance would lead only to futile bloodshed (75)."

While the Danes complied by and large with this ultimatum, the Norwegians offered resistance. Their struggle was spirited but ultimately doomed to failure and Scandinavia, like Austria, Czechoslovakia and Poland before it, fell into the hands of the Reich. During the Battle for Norway, when attempts were made by British troops to rebuff the invaders, King Haakon of Norway and his government were smuggled to safety in the cruiser *Devonshire* and a life of exile in London. Haakon had behaved with dignity and courage, refusing the German demand for the treacherous collaborator Quisling to be appointed Prime Minister of Norway: "I cannot accept the German demands . . . I cannot appoint Quisling Prime Minister . . . If the government decides to accept German demands, abdication will be the only course open to me (76)."

German attacks

By May, 1940, a similar fate was to befall the Low Countries of

Hermann Goering, commander of the *Luftwaffe* (German air force) which prepared the way for Hitler's occupation troops

Europe, Belgium, Luxembourg and Holland. By 14th May the city of Rotterdam, subjected to heavy bombing raids, had capitulated; the Dutch government and Queen Wilhelmina fled to London; five days after the initial attack, Holland had surrendered. Belgium was next. By 20th May the German 2nd Panzer Division reached the mouth of the River Somme, encircling Belgian, British and French forces. General Jodl noted in his diary: "The Führer is beside himself with joy (77)."

Indeed, the Führer might well have been. After all, with little damage inflicted upon his forces, he had succeeded in conquering large tracts of territories, driving back enemy forces, and establishing a seemingly immovable German force in Europe. Even now, he was thinking in terms of a peace treaty, the main provision of which was to be the return to Germany of all the territories "stolen" from it during the last 400 years.

Dunkirk

After the final retreat at Dunkirk, during which an armada of vessels sailing from England began to evacuate the beleaguered armies fighting on the beaches (a total of 126,000 men in four days), it was quite clear that Germany might threaten the English nation across the narrow waters of the English Channel.

On 4th June, in the House of Commons, Prime Minister Winston Churchill made one of his best speeches with this awful prospect in mind: "We shall fight in France, we shall fight in the seas and oceans, we shall fight with growing confidence and growing strength in the air, we shall defend our island . . . we shall fight on the beaches, we shall fight on the landing grounds, we shall fight in the fields and in the streets . . . we shall never surrender (78)."

Dunkirk was followed by the fall of France. Nearly a third of the French Army was already lost and the remaining forces were soon overwhelmed. In June the German Army entered Paris and France was lost. Only a small force of Free French was left, under the leadership of General Charles de Gaulle.

Germany was now left to deal with Britain, a forthcoming battle that Hitler viewed with some regret: "It almost causes me pain to think that I should have been selected by Fate to deal the final blow to the structure . . . I prophesy that a great Empire will be destroyed, an Empire it was never my intention to destroy or harm (79)."

The Battle of Britain

By the end of June Hermann Goering had issued a directive for

Opposite Hitler aimed to cripple British industry by intensive bombing raids

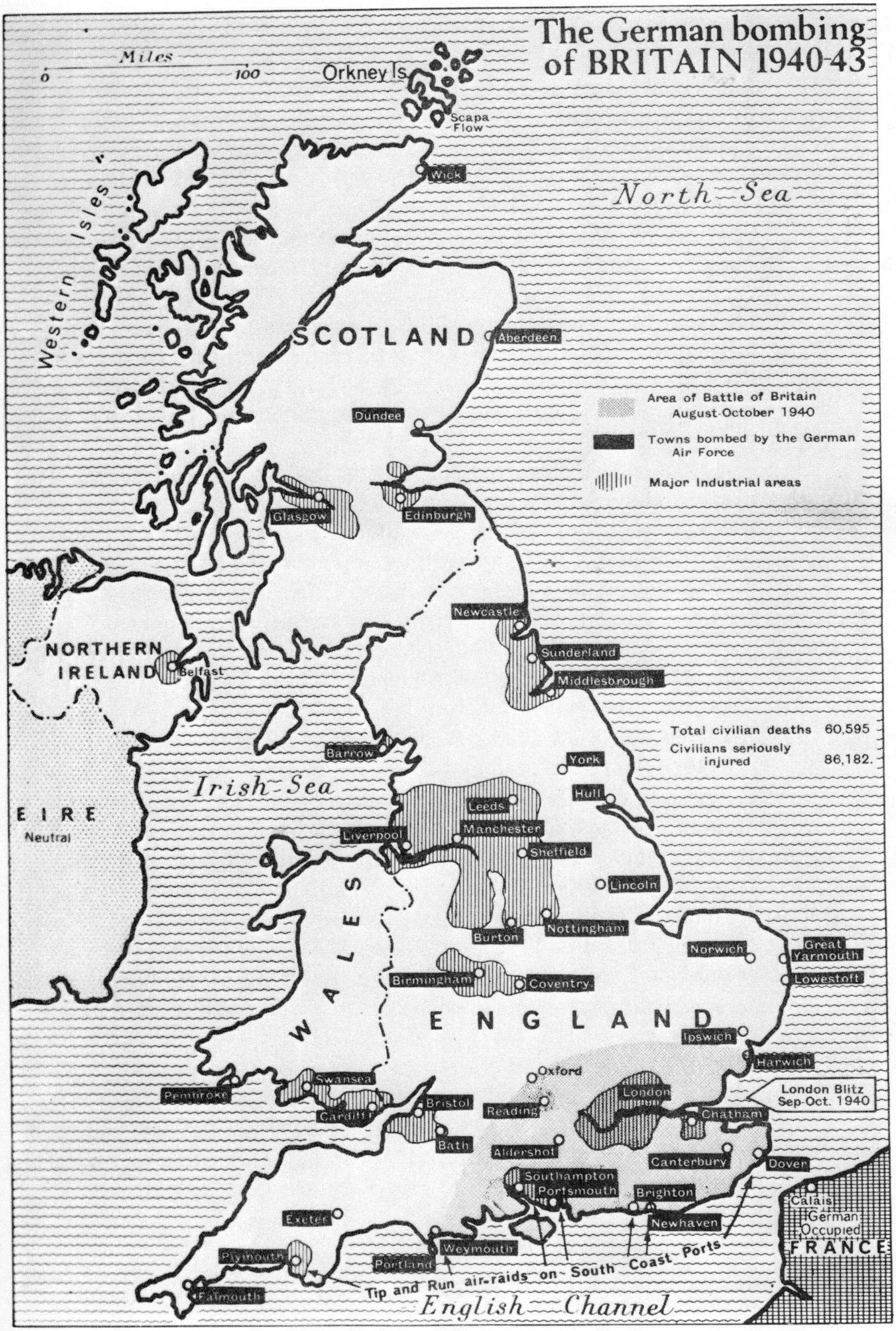

The German bombing of BRITAIN 1940-43
Miles
0
100
Orkney Is.
Scapa Flow
Wick
North Sea
Western Isles
SCOTLAND
Aberdeen
Area of Battle of Britain August-October 1940
Towns bombed by the German Air Force
Major Industrial areas
Dundee
Glasgow
Edinburgh
NORTHERN IRELAND
Belfast
Newcastle
Sunderland
Middlesbrough
Total civilian deaths 60,595
Civilians seriously injured 86,182.
Barrow
York
Irish Sea
Hull
EIRE
Neutral
Leeds
Liverpool
Manchester
Sheffield
Lincoln
WALES
Burton
Nottingham
Norwich
Great Yarmouth
Birmingham
Coventry
Lowestoft
ENGLAND
Ipswich
Harwich
Oxford
Swansea
London
London Blitz Sep-Oct. 1940
Pembroke
Bristol
Reading
Chatham
Cardiff
Bath
Aldershot
Canterbury
Dover
Southampton
Portsmouth
Brighton
Calais
German Occupied
Exeter
Newhaven
FRANCE
Weymouth
Plymouth
Portland
Tip and Run air-raids on South Coast Ports
Falmouth
English Channel

air warfare against Britain: "Active operations against Britain are to be confined to nuisance raids by relatively minor forces on industrial and R.A.F. targets. Such attacks are to be carried out during suitable weather when surprise is possible . . . For the time being heavy civilian casualties are to be avoided if possible (80)."

The objectives of the *Luftwaffe* (German air force) attacks would be: "To create the conditions necessary for a successful campaign against the enemy's war industry and supply lines by defeating his air force, destroying his ground organization, and disrupting his aircraft industry, thus defending Germany's own *Lebensraum*. To dislocate Britain's supplies by attacking ports and harbour installations, ships bringing supplies into the country, and warships escorting them (81)."

By the end of August, 1940, general instructions had been laid down: "The *Luftwaffe* will use all the forces at its disposal to destroy the British air force as quickly as possible. *Luftwaffe* attacks must be primarily directed against enemy planes, their ground organization and their supply system, and also against the aircraft industry, and factories producing anti-aircraft equipment (82)."

Blitz

From August through to November, day and night bomber raids were being made on British targets. The deteriorating weather situation in November put an end to operations by fighter-bombers. And the *Luftwaffe* night raids, made with intense regularity, had not achieved what they had set out to do—namely to cripple Britain and make her ready to accept peace terms. Just the same, invasion plans codenamed "Operation Sealion" were forging ahead: "The earliest day for the sailing of the invasion fleet has been fixed as 20th September, and that of the landing for 21st September (83)."

But hesitation had crept in: Hitler was no longer certain of his ground and seemingly surprised by the ability of the enemy to recover again and again. The invasion was then postponed and the date changed.

Operation Barbarossa

By 12th October, the Führer had gone so far as to change his mind and issued a directive that cancelled the plans for invasion, at least temporarily. Besides, another issue had arisen that was to draw his attention away from the "Battle of Britain". During 1940 Joseph Stalin had moved Soviet troops into the Baltic States.

Although a non-aggression pact existed between the Soviet Union and Germany, just the same Stalin's military maneouvres presented a very real threat to German aims.

And so "Operation Barbarossa" was conceived: "The war against Russia will be such that it cannot be conducted in a knightly fashion. This struggle is one of ideologies and racial differences and will have to be conducted with unprecedented, unmerciful and unrelenting harshness . . . (84)."

Precisely how harsh, Hitler could not then have guessed. And precisely how disastrous for Germany, he could not then have foreseen. By June, 1941, the war with Russia was under way.

Within three weeks German forces commanded by Field-Marshal von Bock, had pushed 450 miles deep into Russia. Moscow was only 200 miles away. Field-Marshal von Leeb's forces were forging towards Leningrad and the army group under Field-Marshal von Rundstedt was moving towards Kiev. It was to be a barbarous war and a long one.

That Hitler had imperialist designs on Russia is apparent from his conversations of the time: "What India is for England the territories of Russia will be for us. If only I could make the German people understand what this space means to our future . . . (85)."

Germany invades Russia

By 2nd October the offensive on Moscow was finally launched. But conditions were bad and the Russian winter was approaching. In his memoirs Field-Marshal Kesselring writes: "The climatic difficulties of the Russian winter did the rest: there was rain and mist and it was very cold . . . No matter how often and resolutely our pilots attacked, the conditions were so difficult that their efforts were never decisive (86)."

By November, 1941, frost was severe. Infantry and horses suffered badly and engines stalled all too frequently. Progress was difficult, often impossible. The 17th Panzer Division had been engaged and held by fresh Russian troops, and Soviet forces arriving from Siberia meant increasing difficulties for the Germans. Near to the end of November the Quartermaster-General of Army High Command complained: "We have come to the end of our resources in both men and material (87)."

On 1st December Field-Marshal von Bock saw how the situation was deteriorating: "The idea that the enemy forces opposing us would collapse is an illusion, as the fighting during the last fourteen days has shown. To remain before the gates of Moscow . . . means heavy defensive fighting against a numerically superior enemy . . . It is therefore difficult to see what sense there is in continuing the operation particularly as the moment is now very near when the strength of the troops will be utterly exhausted (88)."

By the end of February, 1942, the German forces had been driven back amidst fierce fighting and in appalling conditions from the gates of Moscow. Casualties sustained by the German forces in this abortive offensive numbered more than a million men. Bogged down in the spring mud, the German forces retreated and the steam went out of the Russian campaign, to be revived again when summer came.

Battle of Stalingrad

The decisive battle in the summer offensive took place at Stalingrad. Troops of the German 6th Army reached the River Volga, north of Stalingrad, on 23rd August, 1942. The idea of the campaign was that the 6th Army, together with the 4th Panzer division, would encircle the city of Stalingrad, thus enabling the German forces to make another advance on central Russia, and ultimately on Moscow.

But Russian forces had already delivered an aggressive blow to the Italian 8th Army across the River Don, negating a major part of the German offensive. The Italian Army had been protecting the northern flank of the German 6th Army and as a consequence of Soviet aggression, the Führer's plans suffered a setback. Between 1st September and 15th September the Germans moved slowly into the suburban complex of Stalingrad, meeting heavy losses in a battle that lasted for two and a half months.

On 20th November, after bitter fighting and desperate Soviet resistance, two Russian infantry groups advanced to the south of Stalingrad and attacked another force of the German's allies, the Rumanian 4th Army. The previous day the Rumanian 3rd Army had been splintered by another Soviet assault. A German counter-attack was prepared but by 22nd November, as a result of fresh Soviet troops arriving from the north-west and the south-east, the German 6th Army was surrounded. There arose a problem now of supplies, of ammunition and food, and an air lift was operated.

Opposite top The rapidity of German conquest *Opposite bottom* A Russian soldier takes a dead German's rifle during the Russian resistance to Germany, 1942

The GERMAN MASTERY of EUROPE 1942
GREAT BRITAIN
EIRE
North Sea
NORWAY
Oslo
SWEDEN
FINLAND
Leningrad
Stockholm
ESTONIA
LATVIA
Riga
LITHUANIA
Moscow
DENMARK
Copenhagen
Baltic Sea
Danzig
London
HOLLAND
Channel Islands Occupied 1940-45 by Germany
BELGIUM
Berlin
GERMANY
Minsk
RUSSIA
Warsaw
Brest Litovsk
POLAND
Stalingrad
Paris
LUXEMBURG
Prague
Lvov
Kiev
Dnieper
FRANCE
SLOVAKIA
Rostov
Vienna
SWITZERLAND
Budapest
HUNGARY
Vichy
RUMANIA
ITALY
YUGOSLAVIA
Belgrade
Bucharest
Black Sea
SPAIN
Corsica
Sofia
BULGARIA
Rome
ALBANIA
GREECE
TURKEY
Sardinia
Mediterranean Sea
Sicily
ALGERIA
Axis Powers
Powers co-operating with Axis
Territory occupied by Axis
France - Vichy Governed
Neutrals
Unconquered
Miles
0
300

Stalingrad ultimatum

Directed by General Hoth, the 6th Army made preparations for a break-out and by 19th December amidst heavy fighting Hoth's force had fought some way clear. But by 22nd December it was obvious that Russian resistance was too strong: the drive on Stalingrad was to be abandoned. Early in 1943 an ultimatum was presented to the German forces on the northern perimeter of Stalingrad: surrender or oblivion. The winter was harsh, the Germans suffering from hunger, sickness and cold.

The ultimatum was ignored and by 10th January the final phase in the Battle of Stalingrad had begun. By noon on 2nd February, after protracted fighting across the frosted wastes of Stalingrad, the German 6th Army, in a state of utter collapse, surrendered. More than 90,000 German prisoners of war were taken by the Russians.

The tide turns

Elsewhere in the world a watershed in the German military offensive seemed to have been reached. The British-American forces had landed in the desert at El Alamein; by 28th March the Germans had withdrawn from the Mareth line in Tunisia. The previous month, February, had seen the withdrawal of Japanese forces from Guadalcanal. By May the Germans had surrendered in Tunisia. Daily, with terrible regularity, Germany itself was being bombed and destroyed: on the 24th May the R.A.F. reached the 100,000-ton mark in its bomb attacks on Germany.

Life in wartime Germany

So the tide was slowly turning. But while the German military

Above The Germans suffered greatly under Allied bombing attacks machine was slowly being pushed back, what was life like in the Reich for those who had not gone to war? "By the time the heavy English air raids of 1943 finally put a stop to the luxury life, our surface gaiety had worn very thin indeed. It was almost a relief to pack one's suitcase and stop pretending. After the big attack on Hamburg in July, 1943 . . . many of the terrified survivors arrived in Berlin in their nightdresses (89)."

It was becoming a life of constant fear and deprivation: the gilt of the thousand-year Third Reich was beginning to tarnish under the relentless air attacks on major German cities. Towns became ruins overnight: people disappeared under the bomb assaults. "The news from the Rhineland gets more and more horrifying. They say that people sit in the shelters wrapped in wet sheets and wearing steel helmets and gauze spectacles, because phosphorous burns one blind instantly . . . The future is like an approaching storm . . . (90)."

Already the glorious years of the Reich were over. News of military setbacks—gleaned usually from the B.B.C. and not from the propaganda of German radio—had a depressing effect. The landscape had changed to one of ruin. "They say whole districts of Hamburg were a sea of fire. People got stuck in the melted asphalt and stifled for lack of oxygen . . . The lowest estimate is 50,000 dead (91)."

No more joy

For the ordinary soldier, as well as the ordinary person, there was often acute fear. The German novelist Heinrich Böll writes of the young soldier travelling to the Russian front in 1943: "Yes, I'm going to die soon and before the war is over. I shall never know peace again. No peace for me. There will be no more music, no more flowers, no more poetry, no more human joy. Soon I shall be dead . . . The future is without a face (92)."

The effect of the bombing on the routine of ordinary life was far-reaching: "Our flat, which is without doors, windows, heating, light, water, telephone, or gas, is worse than a shanty in the desert (93)."

By the end of 1943 the war had touched everyone's life in one way or another: it was a fact of life from which there was no escape. On the military front there were reverses. Early in 1944 the Russians crossed the Polish border and the Allied Armies were making their

Overleaf The devastation of Berlin after Allied bombing

assault on Europe. The Germans were being driven back out of Russia and by the summer were retreating from the positions they had held in Italy.

The shape of the war was changing. The Soviet Army reached East Prussia in the autumn and almost at the same time Paris was liberated. Even so, Hitler was still rallying hard to salvage the wreck: "Wars are finally decided by one side or the other recognizing that they cannot be won. We must allow no moment to pass without showing the enemy that they can never reckon on our capitulation. Never! (94)."

The Führer trembles

But by the end of 1944 it was obvious that the end was merely a matter of time. Even Hitler seemed to have undergone a physical change: "It was no longer simply his left hand but the whole left side of his body that trembled . . . (95).

In January, 1945, the Russians had overrun Poland and by March the Allies had crossed the Rhine. Germany itself was now ready to be invaded. On 9th April the German city of Königsberg fell to the Russians and two days later Vienna was recaptured. The military setbacks had induced a state of paranoia in the Führer: "I can rely on no-one. They all betray me. The whole business makes me sick . . . I have no successor. Hess is insane. Goering has lost the sympathy of the nation (96)."

By April the Russians stormed Berlin where bitter street fighting took place. Last-ditch stands by the Germans, by anyone old enough to hold a rifle, were both desperate and courageous. Hitler waited in the bunker of the Chancellery for news of fresh forces

Above Germans leave their home town after undergoing shellfire

coming to the relief of Berlin. But there were no fresh forces.

By 28th April Russian forces, having overcome the resistance, were only a few streets away from the Führer's hideout in the Wilhelmstrasse. On 29th April, convinced now that the end was at hand, Hitler wrote out his last will and testament: "It is untrue that I or anybody else in Germany wanted war in 1939. It was wanted and provoked entirely by those international statesmen who were either of Jewish origin or worked for Jewish interests (97)."

Even in defeat, Hitler still clung to his psychotic anti-Semitism. Even in defeat, though, he would remain in Berlin until the bitter end: "I cannot forsake the city that is the capital of the Reich. I have decided to remain in Berlin and of my own free will choose death at the moment when I believe the position of Führer and Chancellor can no longer be held (98)."

Hitler's suicide

Suicide was the Führer's answer to defeat. He would die in order to "escape the disgrace of deposition or capitulation. It is [my] wish to be burned immediately in the place where I have carried out the greater part of my daily work during the course of my twelve years' service to my people (99)."

On Monday, 30th April, 1945, the Führer shot himself through the mouth, although other reports indicate that he swallowed cyanide. The war that had begun so promisingly and aggressively with the march into Poland had ended ingloriously in the shame of suicide.

On the 7th May, 1945, Germany signed an unconditional surrender.

Above Germans, finally defeated, dig for potatoes. The shattered Reichtag (Parliament) building is in the background

Ich bin am Ort
das größte Schwein
und laß mich nur
mit Juden ein!

4 *The Jews: A People put to Death*

German anti-Semitism

ANTI-SEMITISM, which has always met with a response in Germany, reached its peak during the Third Reich. It began with the comparatively mild vandalism of 1933 through the *Kristallnacht* of 1938 to the mass murders in Dachau, Auschwitz and other death camps. Never before has a race of people been so systematically put to death.

The reasons for German anti-Semitism are hard to identify. On the most basic level, reaction to the Jews in the Third Reich was coloured largely by economic considerations. Before the rise of Adolf Hitler the German economy was massively inflated; a not uncommon occurrence was that people took home their wages in suitcases, so low was the value of the paper currency. The Jews, because of their not unnatural clannishness, were singled out as a scapegoat for these troubles.

Jewish poverty

Moreover, it was commonly held that the Jews were far more wealthy than the Germans, a misconception that aggravated an already delicate situation. There were prosperous Jews of course, just as there were prosperous Germans, but it was conveniently overlooked in 1933 that, out of a total of 170,000 Jews, no fewer than 31,000 were receiving charity. The irrational attitudes that arrived with the Third Reich blinded many Germans to the fact that there were poor as well as wealthy Jews. As a people, the Jews presented a convenient scapegoat.

Even so, it is a long way from anti-Semitism to the gas chambers of Auschwitz, and the process a tortuous one. From 1933, acts of vandalism and violence, reinforced by racial laws, contributed to the ultimate slaughter of the Jews; every single act can be seen as another inexorable step towards genocide.

Idea of a Jewish plot

Involved in German anti-Semitism was another stranger reason that we might mention in passing. This was the idea—at one time widespread—of a universal Jewish conspiracy to rule the world.

Opposite A German woman is advertized as a friend of the Jews: "I am the greatest swine in this town, and only get involved with Jews!"

These books were used by the Nazis to try and prove the existence of a Jewish conspiracy to rule the world

The belief first gained prominence in a notorious document called *The Protocols of the Elders of Zion,* later shown to have been a deliberate forgery (100). Only the most rabid anti-Semites took any notice of this nonsense. Alarmingly perhaps, modern editions of the document can still be purchased in many countries of the world, its pages dominated by cruel cartoons. If German anti-Semitism as manifested in the Third Reich contained accusations of a far-fetched Jewish plot, then *The Protocols* are to blame.

Rosenberg and racialism

Another factor in the rise of anti-Semitism was the Third Reich's garbled philosophy of racial purity. Only those of Aryan descent—pure Aryan descent untainted by Jewish, negro, or other alien blood—were good Germans.

One of the so-called "philosphers" of the Nazis was Alfred Rosenberg, later editor of the scurrilous anti-Jewish newspaper the *Völkischer Beobachter (Citizens' Observer)*. Rosenberg published many books including *The Tracks of the Jew Through the Ages* and *The Crime of Freemasonry*. In Hitler's eyes he was the chief ideologist of the Nazi Party. Here is a sample of Rosenberg's thinking: "The conflict between blood and blood represents the ultimate phenomenon accessible to us . . . Racial history is natural history . . . the great world story of the rise and downfall of peoples . . . (101)."

This emphasis on "blood," a curious mystical concept, was to characterize Nazi anti-Semitism. If the "conflict between blood and blood" entailed the supremacy of the Nordic peoples over the Jews, then this barely mattered for the philosophers of National Socialism. The German geneticist, Letz, published these words in 1933: "The aim of socialism [National Socialism, that is] should be the welfare not of the individual but of the race . . . The State is not there to see that the individual gets his rights, but to serve the race (102)."

Threat to Jewry

So National Socialism (Nazism) preached a philosophy of blood purity that excluded the Jews, who were ever after regarded as a tainted race of people. Worse still, the hardness of Nazism—the supremacy of the state over the individual—meant that the Jews could barely expect charitable treatment. Besides, the Jews were decidedly "inferior": "If we stress what Europe owes to the Nordic race, this is not because of some biological evaluation, but because the realities of politics have shown that this race—both in the past and in the present—is capable of unifying the whole of Europe into a single powerful community (103)."

The unification of Europe, then, was something that only the Aryan people were apparently capable of achieving. So far as the Jews were concerned, what could they expect as an inferior race? What did the future in the Third Reich hold for them when its leaders could make such agonizingly pointed statements? "The Jew is not a human being. He is a symbol of putrefaction (104)."

"The fight begins"

That was the harsh comment of the Nazi judge, Walter Buch. Street posters in German cities were equally to the point: "Jews are given until 10 a.m. on Saturday to reflect. Then the fight begins.

The Jews of the world want to destroy Germany. German people! Defend yourselves! Do not buy from the Jews! (105)."

This was no simple admonition to the German people in 1933 to shop only in non-Jewish stores; there were other far more ominous overtones. The April boycott of 1933 was characterized by Stormtroopers (S.A.) picketing Jewish stores and handing out anti-Semitic leaflets. If according to Rosenberg "a new faith is awakening: the myth of blood, the faith to defend, by defending the blood, the divine essence of man (106)"—then it was simply a matter of time before Jewish blood was spilled. The writing was on the wall in more ways than one. The Jewish synagogue in Düsseldorf—like many another throughout the Reich—had the motto *"Jew Perish"* scrawled on its bricks. In a famous photograph published throughout the world, the Munich lawyer Dr. Spiegel was seen walking barefoot through the streets of Munich—followed by Stormtroopers—with a placard around his neck: *"I shall never complain to the police again."*

S.A. quarters in Nuremberg. "By resisting the Jews, I fight for the Lord"

The attitudes of the Stormtroopers themselves naturally varied as to their treatment of German Jews. But the following is perhaps typical: "Naturally you can't help not liking the Jews. They had entered the Fatherland after the war, and had sucked it dry with their foreign money and commercial skill. But I didn't hate the Jews—not all the Jews, although I was quite pleased to see them leave Germany . . . When I sang songs like 'Throw out all the Yiddish gang' and 'When on my Knife the Jew Blood Spurts,' I never really meant all Jews (107)." The slight overtone of self-exculpation must be taken with a pinch of salt. Orders, it was said, were orders, and private attitudes could not influence them one jot.

Anti-Semitic S.S. views

Stormtrooper marching songs of the period are indicative and must have been especially macabre when sung noisily and cheerfully (108):

Hitler is our leader
And spurns their proffered bribes,
He'll kick the faithless Jewish swine
Back to their heathen tribes.

Or again (109):

Load the empty rifles,
Polish the gleaming knives,
Strike down the Jewish traitors
Who juggle with our lives.

Official S.S. attitudes differed only in tone from the hysterical songs of the S.A. even if the language in which they were expressed was woolly and vague. According to Himmler the anti-Jewish campaign "was a struggle between humans and sub-humans (110)," and the Nazi Minister of Propaganda Josef Goebbels said in 1935, "We want no more stupid, absurd statements from middle-class intellectuals to the effect that the Jew is a human being (111)."

Dehumanized, subjected to boycotts and violence, many Jews emigrated from Germany. Some returned between 1933 and 1935, misled perhaps into thinking that the anti-Semitic score had finally been settled and was now a dead issue. But even if the violence of

Der Sturmer whipped up anti-Semitism by cartoons such as this showing the Jews draining the blood of innocent Germans

anti-Semitism sometimes seemed to subside from time to time, there is no doubt that the seed was a growing one. Education of S.S. men, and the propaganda directed at schoolchildren and university students, was beginning to ferment.

Der Stürmer

The notorious *Der Stürmer (The Stormer)*, edited by Julius Streicher—later executed at Nuremberg—was an anti-Semitic magazine. It contained the most crude and simpleminded cartoons and essays. This newspaper grew in circulation between 1934 and 1937 from around 65,000 copies to almost 500,000 copies. A typical *Stürmer* headline was: *The Dead Jew: Fritz Rosenfelder Sees Reason and Hangs Himself* (112).

A typical reader's letter which appeared in 1935 went as follows: "Dear Stürmer, Gauleiter Streicher has told us so much about the Jews that we absolutely hate them. At school we wrote an essay called 'The Jews are Our Misfortune.' I should like you to print my essay. Unfortunately many people today still say that God created the Jews too, and that is why they must be respected. But we say that since vermin are animals they are also destroyed. The Jew is a half-caste . . . He has a wicked book of laws called the Talmud . . . In Gelsenkirchen the Jew Gruenberg sold us rotten meat. His book of laws allows him to do that. The Jews have plotted revolts and incited war. They have led Russia into misery. In Germany they gave the Communist Party money and paid their thugs. We were at death's door. Then Adolf Hitler came . . . Heil Hitler (113)."

This pathetic, garbled, letter shows how far anti-Jewish propaganda affected schoolchildren, and shows too the kind of article printed in *Der Stürmer*. Anti-Semitism flourished not only in the schools and universities, but touched almost every other sphere of German society as well.

Nuremberg Laws of 1935

Just the same, the position of the Jews might have possibly been tolerable if propaganda had been the only weapon used against them. However, it was not to be so. The famous Nuremberg Laws of 1935 relegated them firmly and finally to the status of third class citizens. The Nuremberg Laws—or the Reich Citizenship Acts—contained innumerable laws against the Jews:

"Marriages between Jews and citizens of German or related blood are forbidden. Marriages contracted in contravention of this law are invalid . . .

"Extramarital relations between Jews and citizens of German or related blood are forbidden . . .

"A subject of the State is one who belongs to the protective union of the German Reich . . . Only the subject of the State who is of German or related blood is a citizen of the Reich . . . (114)."

By this legal definition, the Jews were no longer citizens: "No

Jew can be a Reich citizen. The right to vote on any political question is not extended to him and he may not be appointed to any office of State (115)."

In conjunction with earlier legislation in 1933, the Jews were finally *persona non grata* in the Reich. They were barred from commissioned rank in the Army, from legal offices, from the profession of tax advisers, from professorships and lectureships in universities, from jury service, from literature, art, theatre and the cinema.

Similarly they were banned from the medical and dental professions. The German medical profession went so far as to announce in the *Gross-Berliner Ärzteblatt* that "We, the German doctors, demand that no Jew should be permitted to undertake the medical care of German citizens (116)." Even in the harmless field of sport Jewish sporting organizations had their activities curtailed by local authorities who refused them use of facilities.

Hostility to Jewish community

In more mundane, and yet equally significant ways, the ramifications of anti-Jewish legislations were obvious. Notices appeared in German towns and villages with warnings like "Jews not wanted

Jews under the Third Reich soon had to carry special identity cards

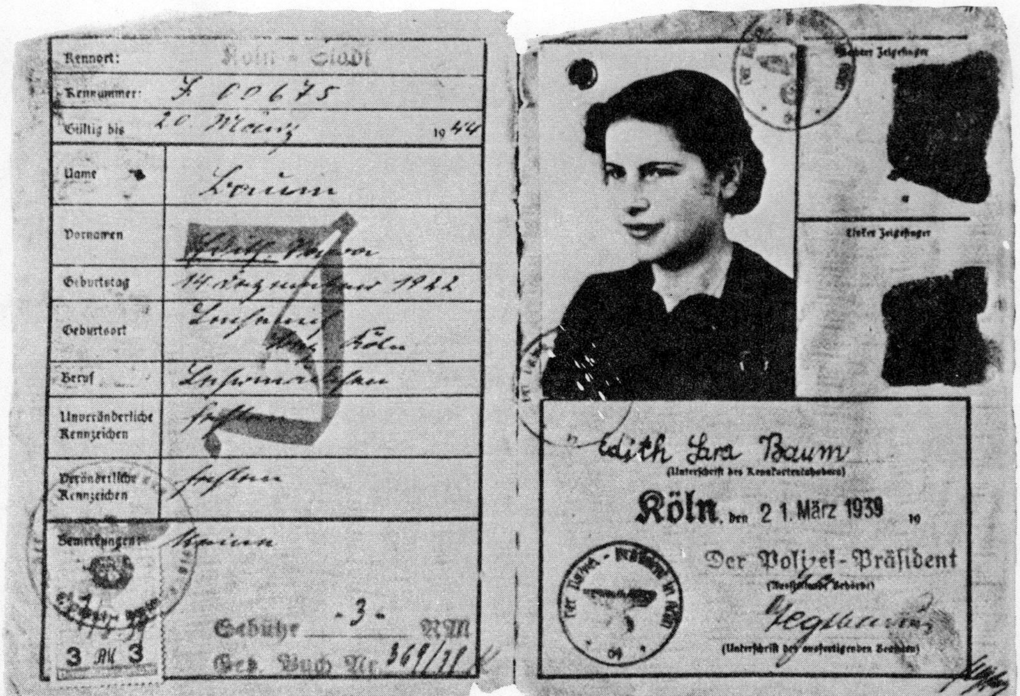
Kennort: Köln - Stadt
Kennummer: J 00675
Gültig bis 20. März 1944
Name
Vornamen
Geburtstag
Geburtsort
Beruf
Unveränderliche Kennzeichen
Veränderliche Kennzeichen
Bemerkungen:
Gebühr -3- RM
Rechter Zeigefinger
Linker Zeigefinger
Edith Sara Baum
(Unterschrift des Karteninhabers)
Köln, den 21. März 1939
Der Polizei-Präsident
(Unterschrift des ausfertigenden Beamten)

Above left A bench in Vienna labelled "For Aryans only," i.e. Jews excluded
Above right By 1941 Jews under Hitler were obliged to wear yellow stars

here," or "Bathing Prohibited to Dogs and Jews." Many Berlin restaurants carried the first notice in their windows. Jewish people were forbidden access to public squares. Municipal parks and public benches were frequently marked "For Aryans Only."

Special identity cards had to be carried, stamped with the initial "J". By 1941 the process of identification had gone a stage further: "Jews over the age of six are forbidden to appear in public without a Jewish star. The Jewish star consists of a six-pointed star, drawn in black on yellow material, with the inscription 'Jew' in black. It is to be worn on the left breast of the clothing, clearly visible and strongly sewn on (117)."

"Night of the broken glass"

Curtailment of basic human rights, suppression to the point of inhumanity, erupted finally into nationwide violence against the Jews during the notorious *Kristallnacht* (night of the broken glass) in November, 1938. The background to the November pogrom began with the assassination of Ernst vom Rath, a Third Secretary in the German Embassy in Paris, by Herschel Grynszpan, a Jew deported from Silesia. This event provided the pretext that was needed for a widespread action against the Jews in Germany.

A teleprinter message from Heinrich Müller, Head of the Gestapo, dated 9th November, 1938, shows clearly what was to take place: "To all Gestapo Stations and Gestapo District Stations:

"(1) At very short notice, *aktionen* against the Jews, especially against their synagogues, will take place throughout the whole of Germany. They are not to be hindered.

"(2) If important archive material is in synagogues, this is to be taken into safekeeping by an immediate measure.

"(3) Preparations are to be made for the arrest of between 20,000 and 30,000 Jews. Wealthy Jews in particular are to be selected.

"(4) Should Jews be found in possession of weapons, the most severe measures are to be taken. S.S. Reserves as well as the General S.S. can be mobilized . . . (118)."

The message ends: "This teleprinter message is secret."

Reinhardt Heydrich circulated to the various state police forces: "Because of the attempt on the life of the Embassy Secretary vom Rath in Paris, demonstrations against the Jews are to be expected tonight, November 9–10, throughout the Reich (119)." And the *Völkischer Beobachter,* commenting on the death of vom Rath, left little to the imagination: "The German people will be able to draw their own conclusions from this new outrage (120)."

An S.S. report

Scenes of violence occurred throughout Germany during that fateful night. Jewish property was destroyed, synagogues burned to the ground. The report of the leader of S.S.-Sturms 10/25 is typical of what took place: "The first measure was the setting on fire of the synagogue in Geldern at about 4 a.m. By 9 a.m. this was burned down to its foundations . . . Simultaneously the interior fittings of the synagogue in Xanten were completely destroyed. Two Jewish shops in the district were likewise completely destroyed. The furnishings of the remainder of the Jews were totally demolished, the windows and window panes first having been broken in. By about 11 o'clock all the male Jews from 15 to 70 were arrested by the police (121)."

Opposite top Shops suspected of being Jewish-owned were wrecked in anti-Jewish riots of the 1930s and *bottom* Jewish shops were marked with the Star of David and the word "Jude"

98.
59.
128

SPEAK ENGLISH

Noticeable in the report is the comment on the passivity of the population at large, a sadly-repeated phenomenon throughout Germany. In Berlin, for instance, the famous Oranienburg Street Synagogue was set on fire and many fashionable shops smashed and looted.

The total of outrages was a high one. More than 7,000 shops had been destroyed; 191 synagogues and 171 apartment houses set on fire, and there was an estimated total of 91 dead. Estimates of prisoners taken into custody—mainly to the Buchenwald prison camp—vary from account to account, but the total is in the region of 20,000.

Goering

Worse was to follow. As a consequence of the *Kristallnacht* the Jews were finally cut off from German economic life. A monstrously large fine was imposed upon them to defray the costs of the riot damage. The notes of the minutes of a meeting in the Ministry of Hermann Goering reveal not only the callousness of attitude towards the pogrom but also the immensity of the fine (122):

Goering: "How many synagogues were actually burned down?"

Heydrich: "A total of 101 have been destroyed by fire, 76 demolished, 7,500 shops destroyed in the Reich."

Goebbels: "Then the Jews must pay for the damage."

Heydrich: "Damage is estimated at several hundred million marks."

Goering: "I wish you had killed 200 Jews instead of destroying so many valuables."

Heydrich: "There are 35 dead" [*An underestimate*].

Goering: "I suggest we use the following wording, that the Jews, as a punishment for their abominable crimes, are made to contribute a thousand million marks. That will do the trick. The pigs will not commit another assassination."

In purchasing power this sum of money has been calculated as the rough equivalent of £100 per head of the Jewish population in Germany.

Goering completed his speech: "I would like to say that I would not like to be a Jew in Germany now. And if it ever happened that Germany should come into conflict with foreign powers, we in Germany would first of all let it come to a final reckoning with the Jews (123)."

Opposite A Jewish cripple being interrogated in Berlin

GIFTGAS!

5 *The Final Reckoning: The Concentration Camps*

Horror in Poland

A VAST LITERATURE has grown around the subject of the German extermination camps in occupied Poland. Vast, perhaps, because some attempt has to be made to understand why and how such things came to pass, how one set of human beings, working with murderous efficiency, could so ruthlessly and cold-bloodedly destroy millions of other human beings. The simplest answer is to say that those who were involved in the task of extermination did not consider that the people they murdered were in fact human beings: rather, they were vermin: Jews, Poles, gipsies—all "non-Aryan" peoples.

Death camps

The final estimate of the dead is unlikely ever to be known with accuracy, nor—when the figure runs into millions—is there any need to know. The entire subject is harrowing and gruesome and there is no need to dwell here on the technical details of the extermination chambers, nor on the so-called scientific experiments conducted on a vast number of prisoners, so painful in their detail. Specifically the death camps were situated in Poland: Auschwitz, Chelmno, Treblinka, Majdanek, Sobibor, Belzec. In the Reich itself were the concentration camps; these were mass prisons, not specifically death centres, although later on during the Russian advance through Poland they became such places. They included Bergen-Belsen, Ravensbrück, Sachsenhausen, Buchenwald, and Dachau amongst others.

The camps were administered by the Death's Head squads of the S.S. Their inmates were primarily Jewish people shunted into Poland from all the Nazi-occupied countries of Europe: from Germany itself, from Belgium, Holland, France, Austria, Rumania and Hungary. For almost all of them it was the end of the road. If by some chance they escaped the gas chambers, disease, deprivation, and torture took their toll of them.

Arrival at Auschwitz

What was it like to be an inmate of a concentration camp? For

Opposite Jews were killed by this gas, Zyklon, in their millions the new arrival at a place like Auschwitz there was the ordeal of selection: "The way we selected our victims was as follows: we had two S.S. doctors on duty to examine the incoming transports of prisoners. These would be marched past one of the doctors who would make spot decisions as they walked past. Those who were fit to work were sent into the camp. Others were sent immediately to the extermination plants. Children of tender years were invariably exterminated since they were too young to do any work (124)." For the unfortunate it was a short road to death. For the remainder it was a reprieved life of slave labour until they became too ill or weak to work any more.

But the selections were an ordeal in themselves: here is an eyewitness account of one woman who survived Auschwitz: "Our turn came. My mother, my sons and I stepped before the selectors. Then I committed [a] terrible error. The selector waved my mother

Jews on the way to a concentration camp where they would be selected either for work or extermination

and myself to the adult group. He classed my young son Thomas with the children and aged, which was to mean immediate extermination. He hesitated before Avrad, my older son. My heart thumped violently. The officer . . . seemed to be trying to act fairly.

" 'This boy must be more than twelve,' he remarked to me.

" 'No,' I protested. The truth was that Avrad was not quite twelve and I could have said so. He was big for his age but I wanted to spare him from labours that might prove too arduous for him. 'Very well. To the left!'

"I had persuaded my mother that she should follow the children and take care of them. 'My mother would like to remain with the children,' I said.

" 'Very well,' he acquiesced. 'You'll all be in the same camp.'

" 'And in several weeks you'll all be reunited,' another officer added.

The main extrance to Dachau concentration camp in Germany

"How should I have known? I had spared them from hard work, but I had condemned Arvad and my mother to death in the gas chambers (125)."

Death trains

Arrival at a concentration camp was usually preceded by a journey under barbaric conditions from distant points in German-controlled Europe. Prisoners travelled like cattle in closed railway trucks. "Inside each of the locked cattle cars ninety people were jammed. The stench of the urinal buckets, which were so full they overflowed, made the air unbreathable (126)."

Many failed to survive, perhaps mercifully: "While we were assembled on the station platform our luggage was taken down by the creatures in convict stripes. Then the bodies of those who died on the journey were removed. The corpses that had been with us for days were bloated hideously and in various stages of decomposition (127)."

What went through the minds of those shunted in such transports? "We travelled in locked wagons, closely packed and half-suffocated. We all said goodbye to each other for we knew that the ovens and gas chambers were waiting for us. Although we often talked about it, nobody could really imagine what it would be like (128)."

Crematoria and gas chambers

Often the first sight to greet arriving inmates was that of the grim crematoria chimneys of the Auschwitz-Birkenau complex: "The chimney began to belch thick clouds of a black, sweetish-smelling smoke . . . A bright sharp flame shot up, six feet high. Soon the stench of burned fat and hair grew unbearable (129)."

The horrible details were often glossed over by the guards: "People asked the guards what was burning, and they replied that it must be bread being baked. Day and night. But we knew that this could not be the case (130)."

Many such attempts were made at disguising the truth. Inmates making the last walk to the gas chambers, stripped naked, believed that they were going to a delousing centre, or were to have a shower. The gas used in the chambers was called Zyklon B, prussic-acid gas. Its production in Europe rose dramatically from 160 tons in 1938 to 231 tons in 1944. In the Belzec death camp the gas chamber bore the inscription, *To the Baths & Inhalation Room* (131)

A good example of the deceit operated by the S.S. as they lured their victims into the chambers is given by S.S. Obersturmführer Kurt Gerstein: "They drew nearer to where Wirth and I were standing in front of the death chambers. Men, women, young girls, children, babies, cripples, all stark naked, filed by. At the corner stood a burly S.S. man with a loud priestlike voice. 'Nothing terrible is going to happen to you,' he said to the victims. 'All you have to do is breathe in deeply. That strengthens the lungs. Inhaling is a means of preventing infectious diseases. It's a good method of disinfection . . .' They walked up a small flight of steps and into the death chambers, most of them without a word, thrust forward by those behind them . . . Many were praying, while others asked: 'Who will give us water to wash the dead? (132)"

A deceit

Most of the inmates knew that they were going to die, to them the deceit was pointless. Gerstein goes on to record the rest of this pathetic, tragic scene: "Inside the chambers S.S. men were crushing the people together. 'Fill them up well,' Wirth ordered. '700 or 800 to every 270 square feet.' Now the doors were closed . . . some Jewish workers on the far side opened the doors. In return for this terrible service they had been promised their lives and a small percentage of the valuables and money collected. Inside, the people were still standing erect, like pillars of basalt, because there had not been an inch of space for them to fall over in or even lean. Families could be seen holding hands, even in death (133)." Could this really be taking place in the twentieth century?

Holding hands in death

How could such scenes be repeated day after day without having an effect of some kind on the S.S. men who operated the death machine? No human being could surely tolerate such events and be unmoved? And yet some claimed that they remained untouched. Camp Commandant Rudolf Höss of Auschwitz seemed to have a somewhat contradictory attitude: "I am completely normal. Even while I was carrying out the task of extermination I led a normal family life and so on (134)." Höss also said, "I never grew indifferent to human suffering. I have always seen and felt for it (135)." Höss's overriding concern was to obey orders: "From our entire training the thought of refusing an order just didn't enter one's head, regardless of what kind of order it was (136)"

The guards unmoved

The figures become meaningless when on this scale

The EXTERMINATION of JEWS 1941-1945
Main German Concentration camps with date established
Approximate Jewish population 1941 (total 8,650,000)
Estimated number of Jews murdered by 1945 (total 5,138,000)
100,000
70,000
70,000 JEWISH REFUGEES TO RUSSIA 1939–1941
2,500,000
750,000
German-Occupied RUSSIA 1941-44
MANIA
1,000,000
750,000
ULGARIA
48,000
40,000
Black Sea
TURKEY
Miles
0 100 200 300

Others were more clearly influenced by what they saw. Kurt Gerstein, for one: "I prayed with them. I pressed myself into a corner and cried out to my God and theirs. How glad I should have been to go into the gas chambers with them (137)." And Hauptsturmführer Kremer noted: "Compared with this, Dante's *Inferno* seems almost a comedy. Auschwitz is not called *the* extermination camp for nothing (138)." In a different but similar context, Oberleutnant Walther observed that after an execution in Yugoslavia, "one or two of my men did not have the nerves to carry out executions over a period. My personal impression is that during the execution one does not have any scruples. These make themselves felt, however, days later when one is thinking quietly about it in the evening (139)."

S.S. cruelty

But generally the attitude of inmates was that "the S.S. were criminal madmen who were not even human (140)." This is hardly surprising when one remembers that the guards were instructed that "any pity whatsoever was unworthy of an S.S. man," and "that there was no place in the ranks of the S.S. for men with soft hearts (141)." Tales of their acts of wanton violence are legion. "I saw those horrible S.S. troops in fits of destructive insanity, blindly beating the sick women, kicking the pregnant (142)." "The S.S. men who stood guard over us would beat us with cudgels and set their dogs on us (143)."

German opinion

What of the German civilian population of this time? Their general attitude seems to have been one of ignorance and blindness, and a later sense of great shock when they learned what had really been taking place under the auspices of the Third Reich. How much ordinary German people really knew will never be clear. Yet the concentration camps of Dachau and Sachsenhausen were close to Munich and Berlin respectively and belief in this ignorance is hard to accept. It is just as difficult to accept their failure to question what they saw in the streets of most German cities—namely, Jewish people being rounded up in public squares and taken off to unknown destinations.

Mussulmen

The inmates of the death camps lived in a state of accumulated numbness. They were subjected not only to physical threats and violent reprimands, but also felt the continual presence of death. Human relationships became impossible; revolt against their conditions almost unthinkable. *Mussulmen*—the skeletal, defeated wretches discovered by the Allied armies in the remains of the camps in 1945—were a new breed of human being.

The horrors of life in a concentration camp

Bodies await burial at Lansberg camp. German civilians dig graves, watched by American soldiers who had overrun the camp

Belsen burials

Corpses were often flung into open graves or large pits and during the German retreat there was hardly time enough for the guards to disguise their grisly tasks: "I cannot very well explain my feelings when I first saw one of those pits which already contained many dead. I had to throw my particular corpse on top of the others already there . . . On many occasions I noticed a strange wound at the back of the thigh of many of these dead. First I dismissed it as a gunshot wound at close quarters but, after seeing

a few more, I asked a friend and he told me that many prisoners were cutting chunks out of these bodies to eat . . . I leave it to your imagination to realize to what state the prisoners were reduced for men to chance eating these bits of flesh taken out of black corpses (144)." Life was not only impossible, it had been negated and reduced to a point that defies description. The eyewitness account above relates to Belsen, but it might have happened almost anywhere.

After death by gassing, the camp victims' corpses were burned in the vast crematoria built for this purpose: "The *Sonderkommando* (*i.e.,* trusted prisoners, often Jewish themselves) tries to work as fast as possible. In frenzied haste they drag the corpses by the wrists. They look like devils. People who had human faces before, I can no longer recognize . . . All the time this is going on, people are being shot in front of ditches, people who could not get into the gas chambers because they were overcrowded. After an hour and a half the whole work has been done and a new transport has been dealt with in Crematorium No. 4 (145)."

Adolf Eichmann

Organizing the concentration camps was an army of bureaucrats, book-keepers in the accounts of death, men whose task it was to arrange the transports and ensure that the death camps were working—like insane factories—to their utmost capacity. Men like Adolf Eichmann, captured and tried and later executed by the Israelis in 1961. Eichmann supervised the great Nazi death department and saw that it continued to function. Yet it remains a curious fact that Eichmann's name was almost unknown to the German population until the Nuremberg War trials. Only then was it revealed that he was the architect, in part at least, of the "final solution" to the "Jewish problem".

"At that time (1944) Eichmann was to my knowledge departmental head of *Amt* IV (Gestapo) . . . and over and above this was charged by Himmler to get hold of all the Jews in European countries and transport them to Germany. He said he knew he would be regarded as a major war criminal by the United Nations because he had millions of Jewish lives on his conscience (146)."

Did Eichmann feel anything? Did he really have a conscience? "I last saw Eichmann towards the end of February, 1945, in Berlin . . . He said he would leap laughing into the grave because the feeling that he had five million people on his conscience would be a source of extraordinary satisfaction for him (147)."

A quibble

In many ways Eichmann was the Aryan bureaucrat supreme. His clerical mentality enabled him to see so many deaths just as figures on a monstrous balance-sheet. He even managed to quibble with Himmler over the exact total: "Eichmann had come to the conclusion that about four million Jews had been killed in the various extermination camps . . . Himmler had not been satisfied

After death by gassing concentration camp victims were burnt in crematoria, shown here

The ashes of the cremated camp victims at Theresisenstadt concentration camp were kept in cardboard boxes

with the report because in his opinion the number of Jews killed must have been greater than six million. Himmler wanted to send a man from his statistics department to Eichmann in order to write a fresh report . . . (148)."

Revolt at Treblinka

But if the machine was run with great efficiency by men like Eichmann, what of the prisoners themselves? It is a charge often levelled against the Jewish prisoners that they went passively to their deaths. Yet what other options were open to them? In the death camp at Treblinka, however, a well-known revolt did take place when 600 prisoners escaped, having first turned on their guards and killed them. It was a rare enough occurrence: "For the first time in the existence of Treblinka, prisoners deliberately disobeyed . . . It raises the hope that everyone will follow . . . The men will leave here with the same message, but the chances of survival in the forest are so slim that it will be by the grace of God if a single one remains alive when it's all over (149)."

At the end of the war, forty of the Treblinka escapees were still alive. In general, though, such revolts and uprisings were almost non-existent. And this is not really surprising. When almost all of one's energy is concentrated on clinging to life for just one day

Living quarters at Buchenwald concentration camp

Camp quarters

more, anger and a rebellious spirit are understandably hard to find.

"On either side of the stove stood three tiers of bunks. To be more exact, here stood wooden cages which we called 'koias'. In each cage, which measured twelve feet by five, seventeen to twenty persons huddled together. Each koia had two miserably filthy, odorous blankets—one blanket for every ten persons. When it rained, the water leaked in . . . There was no floor except the beaten earth, dirty and wet . . . a sea of mud. The filth in the barracks surpassed imagination (150)."

The food matched the poverty of the barracks: "Our first morning meal—nothing except a cup of insipid, brownish liquid, pompously called 'coffee'. At noon we had soup. It was difficult to say what the ingredients were that went into the concoction. The odour was sickening. Often we could eat our portions only by holding our noses . . . Sometimes we fished from the soup buttons, tufts of hair, tin cans, keys, and even mice. In the evening we received our daily bread, a ration of six and a half ounces. The bread was black bread with an extremely high proportion of sawdust (151)." Yet on such diets prisoners were expected to find the strength to work long hours. Failure to do so was punished by death. Typhoid raged in many of the camps, starvation, emaciation, and other epidemics.

Medical experiments

Ironically, doctors were usually attached to the camps, but for other and more sinister purposes. They conducted pseudo-experiments—"high altitude" experiments, sterility experiments, autopsies on twins who had been murdered simultaneously. The horrors of some of these experiments are beyond belief.

The following is a brief extract from the trial of a libel action brought by a London doctor of Polish origin against the author and the English publisher of a novel about the Jews:

Mr. Hirst: "What happened?"

The first man: "They took off the shirt I had, and put iodine on the skin, the left side of the lower abdomen. I saw the doctor putting the iodine on with a swab. After some minutes I saw Dr. Dering when he had my testicle in his hand and showed it to Dr. Schumann, who was present. I felt no pains during the operation (152)."

Recent history

It is hard to grasp the fact that such inhumanities took place in

German concentration camps only a generation ago, or that the men who created the machinery for a whole new concept—genocide—could in so many ways, like Camp Commandant Höss, have been such ordinary people. And yet it happened, and its repercussions are still being felt throughout Europe. In Germany today the law against war criminals has been extended because some of the men who made the death camps possible are still alive and free. They took flight to places like Egypt as in the case of Hans Eisele, the camp doctor of Buchenwald, or to South America like Adolf Eichmann. Franz Stangel, the Commandant of Treblinka, fled to Brazil but was put on trial in Düsseldorf in 1970.

Crimes against humanity

The last word on the subject comes from Sir Hartley Shawcross, Chief British Prosecutor at the Nuremberg Trials. Referring to the twenty-one men who sat in the dock, accused of unimaginable crimes against humanity, he said: "If there were no other charge against these men [*i.e.*, the extermination of the Jews], this one alone, in which all of them were implicated, would suffice. History holds no parallel to these horrors (153)."

6 *Day of Judgement: Nuremberg*

AFTER THE DEFEAT of the Third Reich came the hour of final judgment. The International Military Tribunal was set up at Nuremberg in October, 1945, and twenty-one surviving members of the top Nazi hierarchy sat in the dock accused of crimes against humanity. Hitler, of course, was dead—apparently by his own hand.

Himmler

Himmler, the S.S.-Reichsführer, had managed to commit suicide, thus evading the death penalty that would have been his fate at Nuremberg. He had been captured by Captain Selvester of the interrogation camp near Lüneburg. Captain Selvester described him as a "small miserable-looking and shabbily dressed man." He was wearing a black patch over his left eye, which he removed, "and put on a pair of spectacles. His identity was at once obvious and he said 'Heinrich Himmler' in a very quiet voice (154)."

Fugitives of justice

Josef Goebbels, the Minister of Propaganda, had taken his own life in the bunker of the Chancellery in Berlin, after the death of his beloved Führer. The "blond God" Reinhardt Heydrich was already dead, and Adolf Eichmann had vanished. Martin Bormann who had become Head of the Nazi Party in 1942 disappeared in the wreckage of Berlin and was never seen again (155).

The men in the dock

In the dock at Nuremberg the twenty-one criminals were Reich Marshal Hermann Goering; Rudolf Hess; Joachim von Ribbentrop, the Foreign Minister; the Jew-baiter, Julius Streicher; Baldur von Schirach, the leader of the Hitler Youth Movement; Alfred Rosenberg, the Nazi party philosopher; Field Marshal Keitel; Fritz Sauckel, Reich Plenipotentiary of Labour and responsible for the misuse of labour in the concentration camps; Walther Funk, Reich Minister for Economic Affairs; Schacht,

Opposite Albert Speer, Armaments Minister under the Nazi regime, speaking at Nuremberg War Trials, Germany, where Nazis were tried by the Allies for war crimes

Overleaf (from left to right) Doenitz; Raeder; Schirach (speaking); Sauckel; Jodl; von Papen; Seyss-Inquart; Speer; Neurath; Fritzsche. Front row: Goering; Hess; Ribbentrop; Keitel; Kaltenbrunner; Rosenberg; Frank; Frick; Streicher; Funk; Schacht

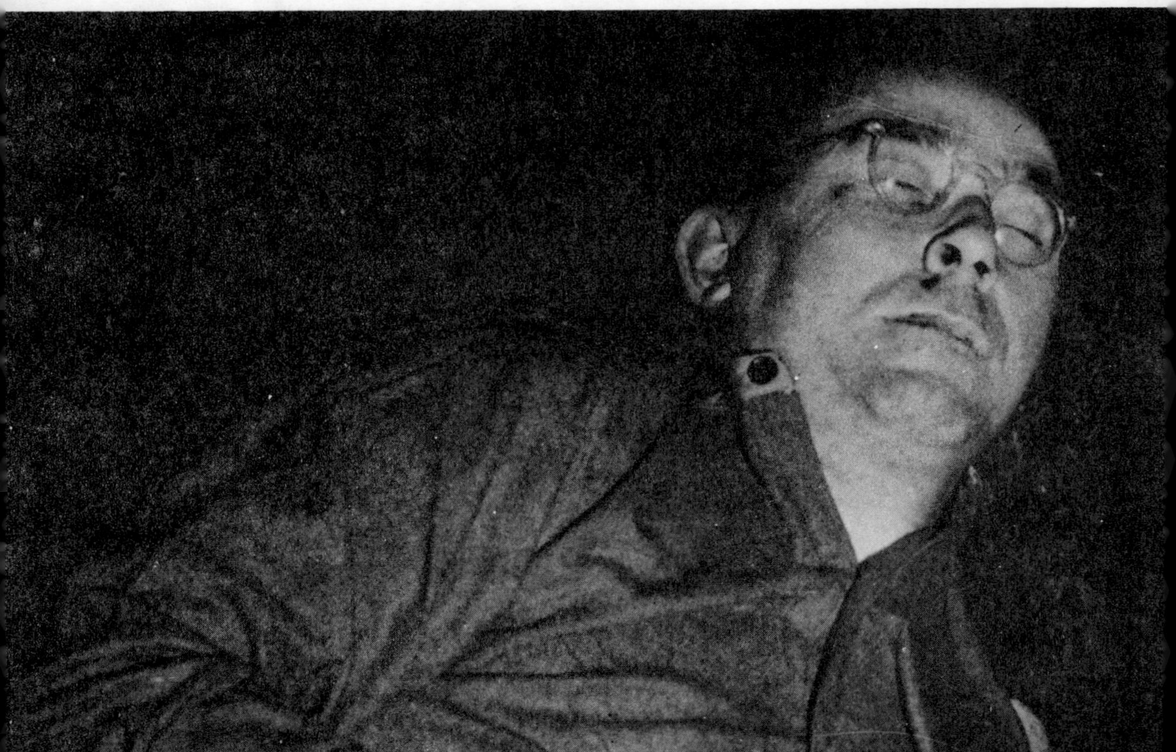

Heinrich Himmler, head of the S.S., after his suicide while being held the Allies

Plenipotentiary for War Economy; Franz von Papen, Vice-Chancellor in the first Hitler Government and later Minister in Vienna; Neurath, Hitler's first Foreign Minister; Albert Speer, Armaments Minister; Seyss-Inquart, Governor of the Occupied Netherlands; General Alfred Jodl; Admiral Raeder; Admiral Doenitz; Ernst Kaltenbrunner, who succeeded Heydrich as head of the Security Police; Hans Frank, Governor-General of Occupied Poland; Wilhelm Frick, the Minister of the Interior; and Hans Fritzsche, an official of the Propaganda Ministry.

Robert Jackson was the Chief United States Prosecutor, and Sir David Maxwell-Fyfe the Chief British Prosecutor. Professor Donnedieu de Vabres represented France on the International Tribunal, and General Nikitchenko was the Soviet Judge. The trial began in November, 1945.

William Shirer was an eyewitness: "I went down to Nuremberg to see them. I had often watched them in their hour of glory and power at the annual Party rallies in this town. In the dock before the International Military Tribunal they looked different. There had been quite a metamorphosis. Attired in rather shabby clothes, slumped in their seats fidgeting nervously, they no longer resembled the arrogant leaders of old. They seemed to be a drab assortment of mediocrities. It seemed difficult to grasp that such men . . . could conquer a great nation and most of Europe (156)."

The indictment

Basically the main charges on which the twenty-one prisoners stood trial were as follows: Conspiring or participating as leaders or accomplices to commit crimes against peace; committing specific crimes against peace by planning, initiating, preparing and waging wars of aggression against a number of states. War crimes—including murder, deportation for slave labour, killing of hostages and ill-treatment of prisoners of war. Crimes against humanity, which included murder, extermination, enslavement and political, religious and racial persecution. The Statute of the Tribunal had been drawn up by the four Allied powers in London during August, 1945.

Arguments on procedure

The articles of trial procedure did not please all of those who sat in the dock: "It is hardly to be wondered at that the rules of procedure seemed to favour the prosecution. Article 3 denied both prosecution and defence the right to challenge the jurisdiction of the Court or its members. This ruled out from the start the possibility of questioning the competence of the Tribunal to deal with the various matters brought before it (157)."

Of the other articles of the Statute the most significant were Article 6, which established the right of the Tribunal to condemn persons for crimes against peace and humanity, and Article 9, which gave the Court the right to declare a given organization—the S.S. for example—to be a criminal one.

Franz von Papen, who sat in the dock, was indignant: "Whenever the defence protested against the unfair advantages which the charter seemed to accord the prosecution, we were reminded that we were lucky to get any trial at all, and that the Allies would have been justified in summarily shooting those whom they considered war criminals as a retaliation for the methods employed by the Third Reich (158)." Not all the defendants shared this view. It seemed, as William Shirer put it, as if no-one "seemed to know why he was there (159)."

Albert Speer

Albert Speer was one of the few, possibly the only one, who accepted that justice had to be done: "I found the position I felt I should take in the trial: to regard my own fate as insignificant, not to struggle for my own life, but to assume the responsibility in a general sense (160)."

Rudolf Hess

Of the other defendants Rudolf Hess was arguably insane, given to long brooding silences, or to reading a book disinterestedly, or to laughing out loud when his book amused him. When called upon to make his final speech, the President of the Court had to interrupt Hess, who had begun to ramble on such diverse and irrelevent subjects as the Boer War and the Church. Even so, he clearly felt no sense of guilt: "I would not want to erase this period of time from my existence. I am happy to know that I have done my duty to my people, my duty as a German, as a National Socialist, as a loyal follower of my Führer. I do not regret anything. If it were to begin all over again, I would act just as I have acted, even if I knew that in the end I should meet a fiery death at the stake (161)."

Goering's suicide

Hermann Goering, the nearest to Hitler of the accused who sat in the Nuremberg dock, "merely fought for his life, using evasions, obfuscations, and denials (162)." He was ultimately sentenced to death, but managed to cheat the hangman by committing suicide in his cell. He had a well-developed martyr complex: "In fifty or sixty years there will be statues of Hermann Goering all over Germany. Little statues, perhaps, but one in every German home (163)."

It was this same man who had so impressed von Papen in his cell at Nuremberg: "He told me that in the latter years of the war he probably felt that Hitler was insane, but he was unable to do anything about it. As a person, Goering had many virtues. He was a man of open masculine nature, with great personal charm. This he retained to the end (164)."

Goering, like Hess, wanted to remain loyal to the memory of the Führer until the end. " 'Not a word against Hitler,' he said to us on one occasion . . . He seemed to think that loyalty to the regime should continue even within the walls of the prison . . . At least it was to his credit that he was the one man who really tried to defend his beliefs (165)."

Joachim von Ribbentrop

Joachim von Ribbentrop, on trial for his life, confronted his prosecutors more melodramatically than some of the other defendants: "I assure you, we were all appalled by these persecutions and atrocities. It is simply not typically German! Can you imagine that I could kill anyone? Tell me honestly, do any of us look like murderers? (166)."

Ribbentrop never really understood what was at stake at Nuremberg. Like a child trying to retract a lie that no-one had believed in the first place, he wrote that, "Truthfully, there was no conspiracy of world Jewry from Moscow, Paris, London and New York (167)." Elsewhere, after the verdict he wrote: "The verdict is utterly untenable. But I was once Adolf Hitler's Foreign Minister and politics demands that because of this I shall be condemned (168)." In the dock, he put up a dreadful performance, described as a failure to convince. "People felt ashamed. The feeling of shame grew, it proliferated, strangled, and cut off the breath (169)."

At the same time, this pathetic creature who had been Hitler's most prominent Foreign Minister, created elaborate defences for himself: "God knows how I fought. It takes less courage to go into battle against atomic bombs than to argue with the Führer on the Jewish question (170)." According to Sir Hartley Shawcross, "never in the history of the world had anyone so degraded diplomacy

(171)." And yet, like the others, he retained a passionate feeling for the dead Führer: "Do you know, even with all that I know now, if now in this cell Hitler should come to me and say, 'Do this!' I would still do it (172)."

Julius Streicher

A similar adherence to the Führer and to Nazism came from Julius Streicher, who had edited the virulent newspaper *Der Stürmer:* "National Socialism is the noblest idea to which a German could devote the strength he has been given (173)." Streicher expressed the deep hope, shortly before his death, that the idea of National Socialism would not be forgotten and would be reborn in a new generation.

Life in jail

The Nuremberg trial lasted for ten months. During that time the prisoners were incarcerated in Nuremberg Jail. They met often and it is interesting to note what they talked about and what they thought as they exercized in the prison yard: "The trial, the indictment, the invalidity of the international tribunal, profound indignation at the disgrace—again and again as we walked our rounds of the yard I heard the same subjects and opinions (174)."

Speer on Goering

Albert Speer is revealing on the relationships between the prisoners: "Among the twenty other defendants I found only one who shared my views. That was Fritzsche . . . Later Seyss-Inquart also showed some understanding . . . With the others, all discussion was useless and wearing. We were speaking different languages (175)."

Speer also noticed Goering's martyr-complex: "He [Goering] observed that the victors would undoubtedly kill him, but that within fifty years his remains would be laid in a marble sarcophagus and he would be celebrated by the German people as a national hero and martyr. Many of the prisoners had the same dream about themselves . . . (176)."

Another aspect of Goering's personality during the trial and imprisonment is revealed by Speer: "Once, in the prison yard something was said about Jewish survivors in Hungary. Goering remarked coldly: 'So, there are still some there? I thought we had knocked them all off. Somebody slipped up again (177).' "

Franz von Papen

Relationships between the prisoners were revealing, but in a different way, from the viewpoint of Franz von Papen: "Frank was convinced from the start that his fate was sealed, that he deserved it, and that his defence was unnecessary. He spent his days in meditation, embraced the Catholic faith, and prepared himself for his Maker. He used to hear mass with Seyss-Inquart, Kaltenbrunner and myself, and I had several conversations with him. He told me he could not understand how he had come so completely under Hitler's influence, or become a willing tool in the criminal persecution of the Jews . . . (178)."

Von Papen had his dislikes as well amongst his fellow criminals: "I had no interest in people like Rosenberg and Streicher . . . . Streicher used to break into loud cries and shouts during the night . . . His co-defendants had little to do with him (179)."

"Schirach seemed to have had second thoughts about the ideals he had impregnated into Hitler's younger generation. On one occasion he remarked to me that he regretted having applied principles which conflicted to such an extent with those of Christianity . . . Speer was full of hope for the future. He expected a sentence of imprisonment . . . (180)."

And as for the wretched Ribbentrop, Shirer describes him as "at last shorn of his arrogance and pompousness, looking pale, bent and beaten (181)." He revealed himself to the world "as what some of us already knew him to be, a husk with no kernel, and an empty facade for a mind (182)."

Defendants' attitudes

Most of the defendants, struggling against what must have seemed the hopeless task of avoiding the death sentence, and with the knowledge that some of the journalists had begun "laying bets on the extent of our penalties (183)," tried to repudiate any responsibility: "Ribbentrop and Keitel . . . whenever confronted with a document that bore their signatures, justified it on grounds of an order from Hitler (184)."

Others tried to shoulder responsibility for what they had done: here is part of a cross-examination between Sir David Maxwell-Fyfe and Franz von Papen: "What I am putting to you is that the only reason that could have kept you in the service of the Nazi Government when you knew all these crimes, was that you sympathized and wanted to carry on with the Nazis' work. That is what I am putting to you—that you had this express knowledge; you had seen your own friends, your own servants, murdered around you. You had the detailed knowledge of it, and the only reason which could have dominated you and made you take one job after another from the Nazis was, that you sympathized with their work. That is what I am putting against you, Herr von Papen."

Von Papen replied: "That, Sir David, is perhaps your opinion. My opinion is that I am responsible only to my conscience and to the German people for my decision to work for the Fatherland; and I shall accept their verdict (185)."

Ten months' trial

But even this acceptance of responsibility shows a certain blindness, a dichotomy between what they saw as duty and patriotism,

Robert Jackson, chief American prosecutor, pictured at the Nuremberg trials

and any sense of morality. As the trial drew to its close, most of the defendants had decided that shame and guilt were perhaps the best pleas after all. Ten months had seen not only the reduction of the defendants from outrage and arrogance to defeat and despair, but there had also been startling revelations of cruelty and murder in the concentration camps that shocked the world. If Streicher could condemn the mass killings of the Jewish community and Funk could talk of his profound shame, if Sauckel realized that he was shocked to his soul by the crimes that the trial had revealed,

Adolf Eichmann, at his trial in Israel 1961. He was the chief architect of the mass exterminations

and Schacht was conscious of unspeakable misery, if Seyss-Inquart now knew about the fearful excesses, and Fritzsche saw the murder of five million people as a horrible warning to future generations—then such confessions came too late to prevent the hangman's rope for many of them.

The trial lasted for 217 days. In 403 sessions three million documents were produced; 80,000 feet of film were shown in evidence; 88,000 affidavits had been signed by 150,000 people submitted for the defence. The offices and partitioned rooms of the Nuremberg Palace of Justice housed about 5,000 people. The team of prosecutors from the United States totalled 600, from Britain 160. The Palace of Justice even had its own restaurant, tailor's shop, barber's, a post office, and novelty shops selling souvenirs of the trial.

The sentences

Of the twenty-one defendants nine were condemned to death: Ribbentrop, Kaltenbrunner, Rosenberg, Frank, Frick, Streicher, Seyss-Inquart, Sauckel and Jodl. They were hanged on 16th October, 1946, less than a year after the opening of the trial.

Fritzsche, Schacht and von Papen were acquitted. Hess, Raeder and Funk were imprisoned for life. Speer and Schirach received sentences of twenty years, Neurath fifteen, Doenitz ten.

An epitaph

It was the end, the fitting finale, to the Third Reich. If an epitaph is needed, it must be the words of Justice Jackson, United States Prosecutor at the Nuremberg Trial: "These two score years in this twentieth century will be recorded in the book of years as some of the most bloody in all annals. Two world wars have left a legacy of dead which number more than all the armies engaged in any war that made ancient or medieval history. No half-century ever witnessed slaughter on such a scale, such cruelties and inhumanities, such wholesale deportations of peoples into slavery, such annihilations of minorities. The terror of Torquemada pales before the Nazi Inquisition.

"These deeds are the overshadowing historical facts by which generations to come will remember this decade. If we cannot eliminate the causes and prevent the repetition of these barbaric events, it is not an irresponsible prophecy to say that this twentieth century may yet succeed in bringing the doom of civilization (186)."

Epilogue

THE REICH lay in ruins. Hundreds of thousands of people were refugees; millions more lay in unmarked graves, the events of their deaths mere statistics in the neat ledgers of the concentration camps; the brass bands had stopped playing, the sign of the swastika had vanished, the S.S. with their dreaded black uniforms were never to be seen again. The moment of barbaric glory had passed, leaving Germany with nothing but wreckage and guilt.

For the Allied armies who entered the haunted land each new discovery of what had really taken place during the years of the Reich was another piece in some terrible jigsaw. Was it possible? How could it have happened? How could Belsen and Treblinka and Auschwitz have happened? What had become of a civilization that permitted a Dachau and a Sachsenhausen?

There are no simple answers. How could there be? To look for a cause in the personality of the Germans is facile and erroneous, since national generalizations of this kind are, at best, primitive. To say that the Germans love order and respond best to discipline and have an unnatural respect for their superiors is really far too simple. What led a nation out of civilization and into darkness is a question that has to be attempted in another way.

Given the social-economic conditions that assisted the rise of the Führer—namely, unemployment, the debasement of currency, the repercussions of defeat in World War One, the years of intense political unrest and warring factions—it is easy to see how Hitler touched some chord in the German people. Out of the darkness there suddenly shone light. The Führer had it in his power to repair Germany and make the nation great again. It was he who would remove once and for all the stain of ignominy caused by defeat in World War One. He would stabilize the economy. He would rid the Fatherland of the twin evils of Communism and Jewry. And, admittedly, these were some of the Führer's aims, and some of his rather dubious achievements.

But somewhere along the way the whole picture changed. It was as if Germany, the nation, mirrored the increasing psychotic state of Hitler, the man. It was as if every deteriorating change in

Hitler's aims found a parallel in the nation. It was as if the identity between the two had become fused into one.

Yet such a thing is not possible unless a nation is in itself prepared to accept the actions of its political leaders. Here we can imagine the value of Reich propaganda. Day after day, in its press and its radio, the German nation was subjected to a barrage of propaganda emanating from Dr. Goebbels's Ministry of Propaganda in Berlin. The Germans had ceased to know exactly what information was true or false. In a sense, it barely mattered. Enthusiasm for the Reich, bolstered by propaganda, had been completely absorbed. There was resistance to Hitler, of course; there had to be. But to resist was to be an enemy of the state. And the state, in Hitlerite Germany, was an infallible institution.

So, on the one hand we have a nation that responds instinctively to its Führer; and on the other we have a Führer whose judgement is believed to be infallible. The consequences—given the personality of Hitler—were disastrous. Added to this were the instruments of terror imposed upon the German people. These were considerable—enough, certainly, to make it easy for people to ignore the whispers they had heard about Dachau, Belsen, and camps elsewhere. The state inspired awe and fear. Too many people had neighbours who were taken away during the night and never seen again.

All of this might effectively have happened anywhere. It might have happened in Mussolini's Italy—except that Mussolini lacked the charisma of the Führer. It might have happened in any other European nation—given the conditions of a depressed Germany in the 1920s—if a Hitler had found his way to power. But history throws up very few Hitlers, and even when it does conditions are not always right for his seizure of power.

The history of the Reich poses a dramatic question for civilization, a question that must one day be answered: are we less sophisticated than the objects that we create? Are we—in an age of television, worldwide communication, advanced science, in an age of ostensive humanity—are we still basically the creatures of the Dark Ages—subjected to primitive impulses and yearnings? In the light of the history of the Third Reich there can be no easy optimistic answer to the question.

Further Reading

GENERAL BOOKS

William L. Shirer, *The Rise and Fall of the Third Reich* (London, 1960)

Richard Grunberger, *A Social History of the Third Reich* (London, 1971)

ADOLF HITLER

Alan Bullock, *Hitler* (London. 1952, revised edition, 1962)

Konrad Heiden, *Der Führer* (London, 1944)

THE S.S.

Heinz Höhne, *The Order of the Death's Head* (London, 1969)

Gerald Reitlinger, *The S.S.: Alibi of a Nation* (London, 1956)

WAR

Winston Churchill, *The Second World War* (London, 1948-53)

Heinz Guderian, *Panzer Leader* (London, 1956)

THE JEWS AND THE CONCENTRATION CAMPS

Gerald Reitlinger, *The Final Solution* (London, 1961)

Karl A. Schleunes, *The Twisted Road to Auschwitz* (Chicago, 1970)

Raul Hilberg, *The Destruction of the European Jews* (London, 1961)

Rudolf Höss, *Commandant of Auschwitz* (London, 1959)

NUREMBERG

G. M. Gilbert, *Nuremberg Diary* (London, 1948)

Douglas M. Kelley, *Twenty-two Cells in Nuremberg* (London, 1947)

PICTURE CREDITS

The Publishers wish to thank the following for their kind permission to reproduce copyright illustrations on the pages mentioned: the Radio Times Hulton Picture Library, 10 (*top*), 14–15, 16–17, 18, 21, 22, 31, 36, 43, 46, 54, 56, 63 (*bottom*), 69, 72, 74, 76, 81 (*bottom*), 102, 104–105, 112–113; the Mansell Collection, 10 (*bottom*), 13, 27, 28, 29, 30, 34, 41, 49, 51, 57, 66–67, 68, 79 (*top left*), 81 (*top*), 82, 94–95, 106; L.E.A., 23; the Trustees of the Imperial War Museum, 24, 48, 53, 87, 93, 97, 99, Camera Press Ltd., 40; Keystone Press Agency Ltd., 42 (*top*), 70; the Zydowski Instytut Historyczny, Warsaw, 78; Centre de Documentation Juive Contemporaine, Paris 86; Pictorial Press Ltd., 84, 114; the cartoon by David Low on page 42 (*bottom*) is reproduced by arrangement with the Trustees and the Evening Standard. The maps appearing on pages, 59, 63 (*top*), 64, 90–91, are reproduced from Martin Gilbert's *Recent History Atlas* (1966) by the kind permission of the publishers Weidenfeld & Nicolson Ltd. The pictures appearing on pages, 2, 98, are from the Nazi archives and were discovered by the Allied troops. All other illustrations appearing in this book are the property of the Wayland Picture Library.

Appendix 1: Table of Events

1933

January 30th	President Hindenburg appoints Hitler as Reich Chancellor
April 26th	Formation of the Gestapo
July 14th	One-party State becomes law
November 12th	First general election: Nazis poll 92 per cent of votes

1934

April 1st	Heinrich Himmler appointed head of the S.S.
July 1934	Night of the Long Knives: the Röhm Putsch
August 2nd	Death of Hindenburg: Hitler becomes overlord of Germany

1938

March 13th	The Austrian *Anschluss*
September 29th	Germany occupies the Sudetenland
November 9th	*Reichskristallnacht:* Jewish pogroms throughout Germany

1939

March 15th	German occupation of Czechoslovakia
August 23rd	Non-agression pact between Germany and Russia
September 1st	German invasion of Poland
September 3rd	Beginning of German attacks on merchant shipping: magnetic mines laid along the English coast
September 8th	German forces reach Warsaw
September 12th	Battle of Kutno

September 17th	Russian Army groups enter East Poland
September 24th	Battle of Warsaw
September 27th	Warsaw surrenders
October 14th	British battleship *Royal Oak* sunk in Scapa Flow
October 16th	German air attacks upon British warships
November 4th	U.S. Neutrality Law becomes effective
November 21st	German Fleet engaged British Northern Patrol South of Iceland
November 28th	R.A.F. raid seaplane base at Borkum
December 17th	The *Graf Spee* scuttles herself, Montevideo

1940

January 16th	Allied preparation for naval/military action in Scandinavia
January 27th	German plan for occupation of Norway and Denmark
February 18th	Combined naval and *Luftwaffe* operations against British-Norwegian communications
March 28th	Allies mine Norwegian waters
April 9th	German troops occupy Norway and Denmark
May 10th	German offensive launched in the West
May 14th	*Luftwaffe* attacks on Rotterdam
May 15th	R.A.F. bomb industrial targets in the Ruhr
June 4th	Fall of Dunkirk
June 10th	End of Norwegian resistance
June 5th–24th	Battle of France
August 13th	Battle of Britain
August 25th	First R.A.F. raid on Berlin
November 14th	*Luftwaffe* attack on Coventry

1941

January 22nd	British capture Tobruk
February 6th	British capture Benghazi
February 11th	R.A.F. raid on Hanover
February 12th	Rommel arrives in Tripoli

March 2nd	German forces enter Bulgaria
April 6th	German campaign in the Balkans begins British occupation of Addis Ababa
April 16th	Air raid on London
April 17th	Yugoslavia conquered by German forces
April 19th	Air raid on London
April 23rd	Greece surrenders
April 24th	British evacuate Greece
May 8th–9th	R.A.F. raids on Hamburg and Bremen
May 10th–11th	*Luftwaffe* raid on London
May 27th	The *Bismarck* is sunk
June 22nd	German attack on Russia
June 29th	Capture of Riga
June 30th	Capture of Lemberg
September 19th	Capture of Kiev
October 2nd	Beginning of the Battle for Moscow
November 18th	British counter-offensive in North Africa
December 27th	Hong Kong capitulates

1942

January	*Luftwaffe* attack on Malta
January 21st	German forces reach El Gazala
May 17th	Battle of Kharkov
May 23rd	U-Boats withdrawn from east coast of U.S.A.
November 5th	Retreat of German forces from North Africa
November 19th	Soviet counter-offensive at Stalingrad
December 12th	Germans attempt to relieve Stalingrad

1943

January	Soviets call on German 6th Army to surrender
January 10th	Soviet liquidation of 6th Army in Stalingrad
January 27th	U.S.A.A.F. attack Wilhelmshaven
February 2nd	German 6th Army surrenders in Stalingrad
March 16th	Large convoy battle: 21 Allied ships sunk by 42 U-Boats

July 5th	Final German offensive in the East launched
July 9th	Allied forces land in Sicily
July 19th	First Allied attack on Rome
September 10th	German troops occupy Rome
September 24th	German troops evacuate Smolensk
November 6th	Russians recapture Kiev

1944

January 4th	Russians enter Poland
January 22nd	Allied troops land at Anzio
March 4th	Russian offensive in the Ukraine
March 15th	Heavy raids on Stuttgart
March 22nd	Heavy raids on Frankfurt-am-Main
June 4th	Germans evacuate Rome
June 6th	D-Day: Allied invasion of North France
June 21st	V-rocket attack on London
August 1st	Warsaw rising
August 4th	German forces evacuate Florence
August 4th	French troops liberate Paris
September 3rd	Allied recapture of Brussels
September 4th	Recapture of Antwerp
September 11th	U.S. Army reaches German frontier
October 3rd	Evacuation of Athens by German forces
October 23rd	Russian forces reach Prussian frontier
December	Final German counter-offensive launched

1945

January 17th	Evacuation of Warsaw by German forces
February 3rd	U.S. bomber raid on Berlin
April 14th	Allies capture Vienna
April 21st	Collapse of the German front in Italy
April 24th	Berlin besieged by Allies
April 30th	Hitler commits suicide
May 7th	German unconditional surrender

Appendix 2: Dramatis Personae

MARTIN BORMANN

Born 1900. Chief of the Nazi Party Chancellery and Hitler's personal secretary. Believed killed in Berlin in 1945, but rumoured to be still hiding in South America.

ADOLF EICHMANN

Born 1906. Representative of Reich Kommissar for the Solution of the Jewish Problem. Tried in Jerusalem in 1961, after a lengthy search, executed in 1962.

RUDOLF HESS

Born 1893. Personal adjutant to Hitler, and No. 2 in the Nazi Party until flying to Scotland in 1941. Sentenced to life imprisonment at Nuremberg 1946, and is still alive in Spandau prison.

REINHARDT HEYDRICH

Born 1904. President of the International Criminal Police Commission; Chief of the Security Police. Assassinated in Prague, 1942.

HEINRICH HIMMLER

Born 1900. Reichsführer S.S. and Chief of the German Police. Suicide 1945.

ADOLF HITLER

Born 1889. Chancellor and Führer of the German Reich. Supreme Commander of the German Forces. Suicide 1945.

RUDOLF HOSS

Born 1900. Commandant of Auschwitz concentration camp. Hanged by the Poles at Auschwitz, 1947.

JOSEF GOEBBELS

Born 1897. Minister for Propaganda. Suicide Berlin, 1945.

HERMANN GOERING

Born 1893. Supreme Commander of the *Luftwaffe*. Put on trial at Nuremberg. Suicide, 1946.

ERNST KALTENBRUNNER

Born 1903. Successor to Heydrich. Executed at Nuremberg, 1946.

HEINRICH MÜLLER

Born 1900. Chief of Gestapo. Believed killed in Berlin 1945, but reported still alive and in hiding.

JOACHIM VON RIBBENTROP

Born 1893. Reich Foreign Minister. Executed at Nuremberg, 1946.

ALFRED ROSENBERG

Born 1893. Nazi Party philosopher and Reich Minister for the occupied Eastern Territories. Executed Nuremberg, 1946.

BALDUR VON SCHIRACH

Born 1907. Gauleiter for Vienna. Leader of the Hitler Youth Movement. Sentenced to twenty years' imprisonment at Nuremberg, released in 1966.

ALBERT SPEER

Born 1905. Armaments Minister. Sentenced to twenty years' imprisonment in 1946 at Nuremberg, released in 1966.

JULIUS STREICHER

Born 1885. Editor of *Der Stürmer*. Executed at Nuremberg, 1946.

FRANZ VON PAPEN

Born 1880. German Ambassador in Vienna, later in Turkey. Acquitted at Nuremberg, 1946.

Notes on Sources

(1) Heiden, *Adolf Hitler* (London, 1944)
(2) Hitler, *Mein Kampf* (various editions)
(3) *Ibid*
(4) *Ibid*
(5) *Ibid*
(6) *Ibid*
(7) Hofmann, *Der Hitler Putsch* (Munich, 1962)
(8) Franz-Willing, *Die Hitlerbewegung* (Hamburg, 1962)
(9) *Mein Kampf*
(10) *Der Führer Persönlich* in *Der Monat*, No. 62
(11) *Hitler's Eintritt*, Deuerlein, 19 & 23
(12) *Der Hitler-Prozess*, Court Proceedings (Munich, 1924)
(13) Heiden, *op. cit.*
(14) Fest, *The Face of the Third Reich* (London, 1970)
(15) Nuremberg Document (1390)
(16) Grunberger, *A Social History of the Third Reich* (London, 1971)
(17) *Ibid*
(18) Speer, *Inside the Third Reich* (London, 1970)
(19) *Dokumente der Deutschen Politik*, II
(20) Richard, *Die Nationale Welle* (Siebald, 1966), quoted in Grunberger, *op.cit.*
(21) Neven-du Mont, *After Hitler* (London, 1969)
(22) Hagen, *The Mark of the Swastika* (London, 1965)
(23) Hagen, *op. cit.*
(24) Wehrmacht WK IX File 137
(25) *Documents on German Foreign Policy (D.G.F.P.)* No. 91
(26) Kardorff, von, *Diary of a Nightmare* (London, 1965)
(27) Bella Fromm, *Blood and Banquets* (New York, 1942)
(28) Gilbert, *Nuremberg Diary* (London, 1948)
(29) *Neues Tagebuch* (March, 1934)
(30) Goebbels, *Michael* (Munich, 1934)
(31) Domarus, *Hitler*, Vol. I (Wurtzburg, 1962)
(32) Fest, *The Face of the Third Reich* (London, 1970)
(33) *Trials of the Major War Criminals* (Nuremberg) Vol. XXXII
(34) *Ibid*, XXIX
(35) Bullock, *Hitler* (London, 1962)
(36) *Der Weg des S.S.-Mannes*, Himmler directive (1935)
(37) Schoenberner, *The Yellow Star* (London, 1969)
(38) *Das Urteil im Wilhelmstrasse-Prozess*, Schwaebisch-Gmuend (1950)
(39) Quoted by Bucheim in *Anatomy of the S.S. State* (London, 1968)
(40) *Ibid*
(41) Neven-du Mont, *After Hitler* (London, 1969)
(42) *Ibid*
(43) Kardorff von, *Diary of A Nightmare* (London, 1965)
(44) *Ibid*
(45) Bucheim, *op. cit.*
(46) Wighton, *Heydrich* (London, 1962)
(47) *Ibid*
(48) Kersten, *Memoirs* (London, 1956)
(49) *Ibid*
(50) Krausnick, *Der 30. Juni, 1934* in *Das Parlament 30. Juni* (1954)
(51) Bracher et, al, *Die Nationalsozialistische Machtergreifung* (Cologne, 1960)
(52) Shirer, *The Rise and Fall of the Third Reich* (London, 1960)
(53) *Völkischer Beobachter* (July, 1934)
(54) *T.M.W.C.* XXI
(55) Himmler, *Die Schutzstaffel als Antibolschewistische Kampforganisation*
(56) *S.S. Liederbuch*
(57) *T.M.W.C.*
(58) Quoted in Shirer, *The Rise and Fall of the Third Reich* (London, 1960)
(59) Nuremberg Documents, C-102
(60) Baynes, *The Speeches of Adolf Hitler* (Oxford, 1942) Vol. II
(61) Shirer, *op. cit.*
(62) *Documents on German Foreign Policy*, DII, No. 221 (H.M.S.O. London)
(63) Baynes, *op. cit.*, Vol. II

(64) *D.G.F.P.* II
(65) *Ibid*
(66) Baynes, *op. cit.*, Vol. II
(67) Shirer, *Berlin Diary* (London, 1941)
(68) *D.G.F.P.* II
(69) Figures from *Wir Haben Es Nicht Vergessen* (Warsaw, 1960)
(70) Hagen, *The Mark of the Swastika* (London, New York, 1965)
(71) *Tria' of War Criminals* (T.W.C.) Vol. XII (Washington, 1951)
(72) *Trial of Major War Criminals* (T.M.W.C.) Vol. X (London, 1946–50)
(73) *Nazi Conspiracy and Aggression* (N.C.A.) Vol. VI (Washington, 1946)
(74) *N.C.A.*, Vol. VI
(75) *Ibid,* Vol. VIII
(76) Shirer, *The Challenge of Scandinavia* (London, 1956)
(77) *T.M.W.C.,* Vol. XV
(78) *Hansard* (June, 1940)
(79) *My New Order* (Hitler's Speeches) (New York, 1941)
(80) Klee, *The Battle of Britain* (London, 1965)
(81) *Ibid*
(82) *Ibid*
(83) *Führer Conferences on Naval Affairs* (London, 1947)
(84) *N.C.A.,* VIII
(85) *Hitler's Table Talk* (London, 1953)
(86) Kesselring, *A Soldier's Record* (London, 1953)
(87) Halder, *Kriegstagebuch* (Stuttgart, 1962)
(88) Bock von, diary, quoted in Hofmann, *The Battle for Moscow* (London, 1965)
(89) Hagen, *op. cit.*
(90) Kardorff von, *Diary of a Nightmare* (London, 1965)
(91) *Ibid*
(92) Heinrich Böll, *The Train Was on Time* (London, 1967)
(93) Kardorff von, *op. cit.*
(94) Fuhrer Conferences, Fragment 28 (12th December, 1944)
(95) Guderian, *Panzer Leader* (London, 1952)
(96) Zoller, *Hitler Privat* (Dusseldorf, 1949)
(97) Nuremberg Documents, 3,569
(98) *Ibid*
(99) *Ibid*
(100) For further information *see* Cohn, *Warrant for Genocide* (London, 1967)
(101) Rosenberg, *Der Mythus des 20 Jahrhunderts* (Munich, 1934)
(102) Lenz, *Die Rasse als Wertprinzip, Zur Erneuerung der Ethik* (Munich, 1933)
(103) *Lehrplan des S.S.-Hauptamptes von 1943*
(104) Krausnick, *The Persecution of the Jews* (London, 1969)
(105) Schoenberner, *The Yellow Star* (London, 1969)
(106) Rosenberg, *op. cit.*
(107) Hagen, *The Mark of the Swastika* (London, 1965)
(108) *Ibid*
(109) *Ibid*
(110) Himmler, *op. cit.*
(111) *Jüdische Rundschau* (July, 1935)
(112) Grunberger, *op. cit.*
(113) *Der Stürmer* (January, 1935)
(114) *Reichsgesetzblatt* (1935)
(115) *Ibid*
(116) *Gross-Berliner Ärzteblatt,* quoted in Krausnick, *op. cit.*
(117) *Reichsgesetzblatt* (1941)
(118) *Das Parlament*
(119) *T.M.W.C.* 3051
(120) *Das Parlament* (1953)
(121) Blumental (Ed.), *Slowa Niewinne* (Warsaw, 1947)
(122) *Dokumente zur Reichskristallnacht*
(123) *Ibid*
(124) Höss, *Kommandant in Auschwitz* (London, 1959)
(125) Lengyel, *Five Chimneys* (London, 1959)
(126) Nyiszli, *Auschwitz* (London, 1962)
(127) Lengyel, *op. cit.*
(128) Poliakov/Wulf (Ed.) *Das Dritte Reich und die Juden* (Berlin, 1955); Esp. Giza Landau, *Im Lager*
(129) Lingens-Reiner, *Prisoners of Fear* (London, 1948)
(130) Giza Landau, *op. cit.*
(131) Friedländer, *Kurt Gerstein* (New York, 1969)
(132) *Ibid*
(133) *Ibid*
(134) Höss, *op. cit.*
(135) *Ibid*
(136) Gilbert, *Nuremberg Diary* (London, 1948)
(137) Friedländer, *op. cit.*
(138) *T.M.W.C.* XXXIII

(139) Schoenberner, *The Yellow Star*
(140) Steiner, *Treblinka* (London, 1967)
(141) Bucheim, *Command and Compliance* (London, 1968)
(142) Lengyel, *op. cit.*
(143) *T.M.W.C.* VI
(144) Phillips (Ed.) *The Belsen Trial* (London, 1949)
(145) *Ibid*
(146) Poliakov/Wulf, *op. cit.*
(147) *T.M.W.C.* IV
(148) Poliakov/Wulf, *op. cit.*
(149) Steiner, *op. cit.*
(150) Lengyel, *op. cit.*
(151) *Ibid*
(152) Hill and Williams, *Auschwitz in England* (London, 1965)
(153) *T.M.W.C.* XIX
(154) Manvell and Fraenkel, *Himmler* (London, 1965)
(155) For speculation on Bormann's fate *see* James McGovern, *Martin Bormann* (London, 1968)
(156) Shirer, *The Rise and Fall of the Third Reich* (London, 1960)
(157) Papen von, *Memoirs* (London, 1952)
(158) *Ibid*
(159) Shirer, *op. cit.*
(160) Speer, *Inside the Third Reich* (London, 1970)
(161) Leasor, *The Uninvited Envoy* (London, 1962)
(162) Speer, *op. cit.*
(163) Kelley, *22 Cells in Nuremberg* (London, 1947)
(164) Papen von, *op. cit.*
(165) Fest, *The Face of the Third Reich* (London, 1970)
(166) *Ibid*
(167) Ribbentrop, von, *Memoirs* (London, 1954)
(168) *Ibid*
(169) Haensel, *Das Gericht vertagt sich* (Hamburg, 1950)
(170) Gilbert, *Nuremberg Diary* (London, 1948)
(171) *T.M.W.C.* XIX
(172) Gilbert, *op. cit.*
(173) Shoenberner, *The Yellow Star*(London, 1969)
(174) Speer, *op. cit.*
(175) *Ibid*
(176) *Ibid*
(177) *Ibid*
(178) Papen von, *op. cit.*
(179) *Ibid*
(180) *Ibid*
(181) Shirer, *op. cit.*
(182) Papen von, *op. cit.*
(183) Speer, *op. cit.*
(184) *Ibid*
(185) Quoted in Papen, von, *op. cit.*
(186) *T.M.W.C.* XIX

Index